BRIGHT NOTES

THE ADVENTURES OF TOM SAWYER BY MARK TWAIN

Intelligent Education

Nashville, Tennessee

BRIGHT NOTES: The Adventures of Tom Sawyer
www.BrightNotes.com

No part of this publication may be used or reproduced in any manner whatsoever without written permission, except in the case of brief quotations in critical articles and reviews. For permissions, contact Influence Publishers http://www.influencepublishers.com.

ISBN: 978-1-645423-34-8 (Paperback)
ISBN: 978-1-645423-35-5 (eBook)

Published in accordance with the U.S. Copyright Office Orphan Works and Mass Digitization report of the register of copyrights, June 2015.

Originally published by Monarch Press.
Alexander J. Butrym, 1965
2019 Edition published by Influence Publishers.

Interior design by Lapiz Digital Services. Cover Design by Thinkpen Designs.

Printed in the United States of America.

Library of Congress Cataloging-in-Publication Data forthcoming.
Names: Intelligent Education
Title: BRIGHT NOTES: The Adventures of Tom Sawyer
Subject: STU004000 STUDY AIDS / Book Notes

CONTENTS

1) A Biographical Sketch of Mark Twain — 1

2) An Overview The Adventures of Tom Sawyer — 8

3) Textual Analysis
   - Chapters 1–6 — 23
   - Chapters 7–11 — 45
   - Chapters 12–21 — 58
   - Chapters 22–26 — 78
   - Chapters 27–30 — 93
   - Chapters 31–35 — 107

4) Critical Battle Over Mark Twain's Psyche — 120

5) Critical Commentary — 131

6) Essay Questions and Answers — 138

7) Subject Bibliography and Guide to Research Papers — 145

A BIOGRAPHICAL SKETCH OF MARK TWAIN

INTRODUCTION

The story of Mark Twain's life is typical of the success stories written by Horatio Alger, the boys' novelist, for Twain had to struggle with an environment that seemed to be against him from the beginning. Born Samuel Langhorne Clemens in the one-horse village of Florida, Missouri, in 1835, he rose to become a world famous writer, lecturer and traveler before he died in 1910. Most of his success stemmed from a combination of indomitable drive, unceasing energy and maximum use of his own talents. He did have some good luck, too, and that helped.

EARLY LIFE

The facts of Twain's life are well known. Four years after he was born the family moved to Hannibal, Missouri — a village larger — but not a great deal different from — his birthplace. During his boyhood he had all the advantages and disadvantages of growing up in a country environment. He was close to the Mississippi River, and probably spent a lot of time exploring its wooded shores and islands. He grew up in tune with the life around him, swimming and playing hooky from school, falling in love, and reading adventure stories. His family was an intelligent though not a wealthy or successful one by any material standards. Upon his father's death in 1847 Sam Clemens was apprenticed to his brother Orion, who owned a local printing shop and a newspaper. (Neither Orion, nor Twain's other brother, Henry, was able to break out of the poverty to which their impulsive and "wishful-thinking" schemes to make big money fast had doomed them.) Sam, however, left Hannibal to follow his trade over a good part of the country, working in towns as different as Keokuk and New York. But the pay wasn't too good for printers in those days, so he thought he'd go to South America and look for gold, or find some other way of making a quick fortune. Had he been successful in leaving the U.S., we would probably never have heard more of him.

LIFE ON THE MISSISSIPPI

Fortunately for American literature, however, Sam never took ship at New Orleans. He had become friendly with a river pilot named Horace Bixby, who promised to teach him about the Mississippi River. Bixby was a good pilot, one who loved his work and established a reputation for excellence. The story of Twain's apprenticeship is told in *Life on the Mississippi,* where he recounts his sudden awakening to the fact that pilots of river boats did more than just stand around looking "gaudy" after the boat had pulled into a landing. If, however, the romantic image of the pilot was gone from Twain's experience forever, it was replaced by an appreciation of the deep beauties of the river, its many shifts and changes, different at various times of the day, and sometimes unrecognizable from one season to the next. The account Twain leaves us is "stretched" somewhat, as Huck Finn would say, but in general the impression it creates is a true one.

LATER TRAVELS

After piloting the river steamers for about four years, Clemens retired to the Nevada gold country because the onset of the Civil War had put an end to river commerce. He prospected and clerked, doing many things to keep body and soul together. Eventually he ended up back in the printing trade, working his way from town to town before more or less settling down in California. He wrote short pieces for the newspapers he worked on, establishing a reputation as a humorist among the provincial readers of the Old West. So successful were these pieces, generally burlesques of social customs and institutions, that his newspaper sent him on a tour of the Sandwich Islands, as Hawaii was called in those days. He wrote a series of travel-letters burlesquing the typical travelogues tourists and professional travelers were sending back to their home towns from abroad. The result of this writing and some lecturing was that he began to be known as an earthy humorist, and classed among such writers as Bret Harte, Artemus Ward, and Petroleum V. Nasby. These men were known for their extremely popular western tales woven from folk stories and written in dialect with rough-hewn humor and plenty of recognizable concrete detail.

THE INNOCENTS ABROAD

In 1869 he published *The Innocents Abroad,* an account of a trip to Europe made under the sponsorship of a newspaper. In this book, he satirizes the folly of going across the Atlantic to see dead men's graves when there were many more living things to see in America, a dynamic and growing nation in contrast to decaying and dying Europe. The book made him famous, and gave him a literary reputation in the East. This reputation opened to him the doors of the cultivated and genteel literary patrons who generally scorned the writings of the Western humorists.

MARRIAGE

As a successful writer he attained respectability enough to marry into a wealthy Buffalo, New York, family. His wife was Olivia Langdon, of the socially prominent Langdons. Many aspects of their courtship, preserved for us in Twain's letters to Olivia and to her friends, remind us of the courtship of Tom and Becky in *Tom Sawyer*. Twain depended on "Livy" to read and censor his manuscripts before they were sent to the printer to make certain they contained nothing that would be improper among the social class he was now a member of. Some critics hold that this censorship did Twain a great deal of harm; others, who examined the surviving manuscripts, point out that "Livy" generally did not suggest more than minor changes, none of which significantly altered the books in question.

Five years after his marriage, Twain moved to Elmira, New York, and then to Hartford, Connecticut, where he had his famous and unusual house, an obvious status symbol, built. Most of his time was taken up with writing, although he did become involved in several get-rich-quick business enterprises that from then until the end of his life drained his energy and his finances, with the loss of not only most of his fortune but of "Livy's" as well.

FRIENDSHIP WITH DEAN HOWELLS

Twain had made friends with a number of interesting literary people, among them William Dean Howells, the famous author (*The Rise of Silas Lapham*) and editor (*The Atlantic Monthly*). Howells was quick to see and appreciate Twain's talent for humor, and encouraged him to develop the talent by acting as his literary adviser and practically guaranteeing Twain the critical backing of the prestigious *Atlantic*.

During this period he wrote *Roughing It* and *The Gilded Age*. The former is a memoir of the early days of the West; the latter, written in collaboration with Charles Dudley Warner, another friend, is a satire on the way the federal government was run in those days. By 1875 he was working sporadically on his first full length novel, *Tom Sawyer*.

HUCKLEBERRY FINN

The only other book that earned Twain more money than *Tom Sawyer* was its sequel, *Huckleberry Finn*. He began writing Huck Finn's story in 1876, and although this is the work on which the largest proportion of his literary fame rests, he found writing it to be hard going. The book was laid aside several times, but each time it was picked up again and brought a little nearer to completion. It did not appear until 1884 in England and 1885 in America. It was an immediate success, despite adverse criticism by some of the more conservative literary judges of the day who felt it was vulgar and dealt with insignificant material.

OTHER WRITINGS

Between 1876 and 1885 Twain had written several books, among them *The Prince and the Pauper, A Tramp Abroad,* and *Life on the Mississippi*. The first of these is a children's book which has as its basic plot a fictitious story of mistaken identity in which Edward VI of England is replaced on the throne by Tom Canty, a commoner. A thoroughly delightful book, *The Prince and the Pauper* was never one of Twain's more financially successful works. *A Tramp Abroad* is another travel book, this time recounting Twain's walking tour through Europe. And *Life on the Mississippi* is an account of Twain's visit to the scene of his early piloting days some twenty-five to thirty years after he left the trade. The work contains a great deal of pleasant reminiscence, social criticism, and much autobiographical material.

After *Huckleberry Finn,* Twain's next major work was *Pudd'n- head Wilson* (1889), a novel which has been published under the title *Natural Son,* which should give you some idea of its contents. Then came *A Connecticut Yankee in King Arthur's Court* (1894), a story about a Yankee engineer who goes back in time and becomes an adviser to King Arthur, enemy to Merlin, and—for all practical purposes—ruler of England until his reforms and charities are overthrown by the ignorant masses led by superstitious knights and clergy.

FINAL YEARS

Mark Twain's final years were not full of the satisfactions a man hopes to enjoy at the end of a life well led. Instead, he suffered a series of financial disasters and personal losses which would have taken the heart out of a lesser man. His publishing company failed in 1894 in spite of early successes — it had paid General Grant's widow $200,000, the largest payment in advance royalties ever paid, and it had reaped much from Twain's own works. Twain also invested a great deal of money in a typesetting machine invented and designed by a man named Paige who did not have to work too hard to convince ex-printer Twain of the need for such an invention. Unfortunately, Paige stretched out the development of the machine, making costly changes and modifications that not only ran up the expenses, but delayed the finishing of the invention until Mergenthaler had produced his Linotype. Twain lost his proverbial shirt.

In spite of his advanced years—he was in his sixties—Twain undertook a foreign lecture tour to pay back every cent he owed. Since he was paid about $1,000 a night, it was not long before he was out of debt. But before he finished the tour, in 1898, there began for him a series of losses that were to color the rest of his life. These were deeper losses, more personally tragic than mere financial ruin. First, his daughter Suzy died, then his wife died, then his daughter Clara went with her husband to live in Europe. This left him with only his daughter Jean, whose epilepsy resulted in a fatal heart attack in 1910. Twain was now bereft of the company he enjoyed most, his girlish family. Four months after Jean's death, on April 21, 1910, Mark Twain suffered a heart attack and died. Disillusioned by business reversals and personal losses, he was a bitter writer toward the end of his days. The acidity of his earlier works was sweet when compared to his later bitterness, which became a violent cynicism and materialistic humanism. Some of his later writings, withheld from the public by his estate because of the savage nature of their biting satire, are just being published.

EVALUATION

His writings, from the earliest to those now appearing, can best be described as "iconoclastic." Twain delighted in shattering the images of glamor and romance built up around what he regarded as false and villainous institutions and customs. As a satirist attacking fraudulent pursuits and the weak, insipid facades of hypocrisy, Twain was a terrible enemy to injustice and confusion.

Many of his attacks seem unreasonable to us with sixty or seventy years of hindsight from which to judge. But Twain's attitudes were colored not only by his times and his lack of formal training, but also by his personality, which has been described by one critic as that of "neurotic genius."

THE ADVENTURES OF TOM SAWYER

AN OVERVIEW

The events of Tom Sawyer happen before those of Huck Finn. The story of Tom Sawyer deals with the misadventures, really, of several children in the little Missouri village of St. Petersburg, about thirty years before the Civil War. The story takes place, that is, sometime during the 1830s.

As the story opens we get a picture of Tom Sawyer, his half-brother Sid and his Aunt Polly. Tom is not the "Model Boy" of the village, nor does he want to be. As a matter of fact, Tom seems to enjoy being in trouble: he's in it so often. At this point, he winds up having to work all day Saturday because he took off from school, and didn't get home until late at night. But Tom doesn't worry over his troubles; he often develops new interests to tide him over periods when he's being punished and life is difficult.

As a punishment, Tom has to whitewash the fence, a chore he finds very distasteful. By pretending the chore is fun, though, Tom persuades his friends - Ben Rogers, Billy Fisher, Johnny Miller, and all the rest - to whitewash the fence. Not only that, but by pretending he wants to do all the work himself, Tom gets the boys to trade him odds-and-ends of things for the privilege of doing his work. When the job is done, Aunt Polly also rewards him for doing such good work.

Then Tom goes out to play with Joe Harper, his "bosom friend." They play war for a while, until time to go home. On his way home, Tom catches his first sight of Becky Thatcher. He falls in love with her, forgetting his love for Amy Lawrence. He shows off for a while, but goes home when Becky doesn't come out of the house after she throws him a flower. When he gets home, he has another encounter with Sid, who told on him the day before and got him into trouble. Tom and Sid don't seem to get along too well; Sid seems to be looking for chances to ingratiate himself with Aunt Polly at Tom's expense. Tom, of course, gets even with Sid every time he can.

In Sunday School the next day, Tom gets a chance to show off in front of Becky and her great and famous father, Judge Thatcher. Tom has traded other boys some of the "riches" he accumulated the day before, and received Bible tickets from them. These are tickets that are given out for memorizing verses of the Bible. When anyone has accumulated tickets that show he's memorized two thousand verses of the Bible, he's called up to the front of the room and given a prize: a copy of the Bible. Tom, who doesn't want to bother learning the verses, covets the Bible because he yearns for the fuss and notoriety of getting up in front of everybody to receive his prize. By trading wisely, Tom has managed to be the only one in Sunday School who has enough tickets to qualify for the Bible. The Judge makes a fuss over Tom - which Tom enjoys - and asks him who the first two Apostles were. Tom doesn't know. He guesses David and Goliath. We don't know what happens next; Mark Twain says only: "Let us draw the curtain of Charity over the rest of the scene."

TOM AND HUCKLEBERRY FINN

On Monday morning Tom tries to get out of going to school, but Aunt Polly pulls the tooth he complains about, and sends him anyway. He runs into Huckleberry Finn, the son of the village drunkard, who is carrying a dead cat he got a week ago. Tom is intrigued by this treasure and asks what it's good for. Huck replies that it's good to take warts off, providing you go about it right.

By the time Tom gets to school it's very late. In order to get to sit with Becky Thatcher, Tom confesses that he's late because he stopped to talk with Huckleberry Finn. He is severely punished for fraternizing with the worthless Huck, and gets his wish - he must sit with the girls. The only vacant seat is the one next to Becky. He manages to make friends with her, and is so overwhelmed with love that he botches his lessons all day. During the break for lunch, he and Becky stay behind and promise their love to each other. But Tom makes the unforgivable mistake of mentioning his old girlfriend. Becky reacts as most women do - she hates him. Eventually Tom reacts as boys do. He tries to make her stop crying by offering her his greatest treasure, the brass knob off an old fireplace andiron. She refuses his gift, but he leaves it behind for her, and he plays hooky for the rest of the day. He wanders about the woods in a melancholy mood for a while, thinking that he will become a pirate. Soon Joe Harper shows up, and the two boys play "Robin Hood."

That night Huck Finn calls for Tom, and they go to the graveyard to have a try at removing warts with the dead cat. They hope to find devils, but instead, they come upon Injun Joe, a "murderin' half-breed." Injun Joe is there with Muff Potter, stealing a corpse under the supervision of young Doctor Robinson. There is an argument about money, and in the ensuing violence, Potter is knocked unconscious, and Injun Joe stabs the doctor with Potter's knife. The boys run away in fear, and do not see Injun Joe put the bloody knife in Potter's hand. When Potter comes to, Joe promises to help him escape and not to tell that he killed the doctor.

Huck and Tom, meanwhile, get to the tannery, where in fear of their lives they write an oath to keep "mum." They sign the oath in blood. Before long they hear a dog howling; the sign is obvious: someone will die. Then a new noise catches their attention. They follow it and come upon Muff Potter snoring. They are sure the dog is howling a warning that Muff will die. The boys separate; Tom goes home, He is unaware, when he climbs in the window, that Sid is awake. The next morning everybody in the house knows that he was out all night. Aunt Polly only makes him feel worse by not whipping him. When he gets to school, he finds his brass andiron knob in his desk. His heart is heavy with sorrow.

That afternoon the village learns of the murder. Potter's knife is found, and he's convicted by popular opinion before he's even caught. He comes into town and is taken by the sheriff, and accused of the crime by Injun Joe. Tom and Huck almost let out their secret. They don't want to see an innocent man hanged. But because they are afraid of what Injun Joe will do to them if they tell, they restrain themselves.

Tom's conscience bothers him so much he tosses and talks in his sleep, keeping Sid awake. Tom is bothered so much by this trouble that he won't join the other boys in holding inquests on dead cats - a new fad which results from the sensation caused by the inquest on Dr. Robinson. (Sid notes that Tom is acting funny by not taking an interest in these things.) In order to ease his conscience, Tom takes odds and ends of things to Muff in the jail. Nobody's going to do anything to Injun Joe, in spite of his grave robbing, because everybody in the village is afraid of him.

In addition to this problem, Tom is troubled by the fact that Becky Thatcher is ill and isn't coming to school. He loses interest in everything - piracy, hoops, war, and all - so much so that

Aunt Polly is afraid he's sick and begins feeding him all kinds of patent medicines an trying all new "cures" on him. One day Tom feeds some Pain Killer to the cat, and the cat practically tears the room apart in a frenzy. Aunt Polly asks Tom why he did it, and Tom replies that he did it because he felt sorry for the cat who doesn't have an Aunt to torment it with all kinds of medicines and cures. Polly takes him off the medicines and things; this is a great relief to him.

When Becky gets back to school, Tom is overjoyed. He shouts and leaps about, but to no avail. For when he is near her, Becky says to someone else: "Mf! some people think they're mighty smart -always showing off!" Tom decides to lead a life of crime. Feeling sorry for himself, he plays hooky again. He meets Joe Harper again, and they plan to go over to Jackson's Island - about three miles below St. Petersburg - and live as pirates. They take Huck Finn with them when they go over that night. Huck enjoys being out that way. But Tom and Joe can't sleep. Their consciences bother them for running away from home.

The next day the ferryboat comes out, its cannon booming, to drop loaves with quicksilver in them in an attempt to recover the bodies of the boys, whom the villagers believe to be drowned. Joe wants to go home, but Tom ridicules him scornfully. That night Tom goes over to the village, stops at his Aunt's house where Polly, Sid, Mary, and Joe Harper's mother are gathered, talking. He hides where he can overhear the conversation. They are talking about the boys; Aunt Polly thinks highly of Tom - now that he's "gone". The work is that if the boys or their bodies are not recovered by Sunday morning, the funerals will be held that afternoon without the bodies.

Tom sneaks back to the island, getting there just as Joe and Huck are discussing his disappearance. He tells them of his adventures during the night, and goes to sleep. Later on, in order to keep the others from going home, Tom tells them his secret plan. They decide to stick together, since they have the marvelous secret, and can laze around and "smoke and chatter and brag."

There was no joy or comfort in the village, though. Everyone was sorry for the deaths of the boys. Becky Thatcher wished she hadn't given the knob back to Tom. After the Sunday School next day, the bell tolls for the funeral service. As things go along, there is a rustle in the gallery. It's the three boys; they've been hiding in the gallery listening to their own funeral services! The welcome they receive is the most exciting ever. And Tom basks in the glow of attention he is getting. A regular hero, he feels he no longer needs Becky Thatcher. But Becky wants him back. To gain his attention she talks loudly about a picnic she's going to have along about vacation time. But Tom pretends not to notice or care. He starts paying attention to Amy Lawrence. Becky gets revenge by ignoring Tom in favor of some other boy. Tom sees this and gets downhearted. He goes home. As soon as she notices that Tom isn't around any longer, she chases the other boy away. He understands that Becky's been using him to get back at Tom, and he is angry. He decides to get Tom in trouble by spilling ink on Tom's spelling book. Becky happens to pass the schoolroom window at the time, and she sees him. But she decides not to tell Tom because she's still angry with him for the way he behaved when she was talking about her picnic.

While he's at home for lunch, Tom talks with his Aunt Polly about his escapade on Jackson's Island, and about the visit he made to the house that one night. He and Aunt Polly are happy, so happy, in fact, that she kisses him, making him feel good. He is feeling so good that when he gets back to school he apologizes to Becky. But Becky, realizing she has the upper hand now, acts cold toward him.

Before afternoon classes begin, Becky has a chance to sneak into the classroom and take a peek at the book the teacher keeps locked in his desk. While she's there, engrossed in the book - it's an anatomical textbook - Tom comes into the room, surprising her. In her hurry to put the book away, she tears a page. She's sure she'll be whipped in class, and she's horrified at the thought. Tom thinks she's a regular milksop for worrying about a little caning. After all, he's been whipped in class many times and it never bothered him. Although he's sorry for her, he has too many of his own problems to worry about. The teacher discovers Tom's ink-stained spelling book, and punishes him. Tom doesn't think twice about the whipping he gets; it's all in a day's work, and besides he just might have spilled the ink without realizing it.

A little while later, the teacher takes his book out to read for a while. He notices the torn page, and asks each child - beginning with the girls - whether she tore the page. Just as he gets to Becky Thatcher, Tom jumps up and says he tore the page. He takes the whipping Becky would have got, in order to keep her from being embarrassed in front of the class. Becky is grateful, and loves Tom even more than she did before - for his nobility.

Just before vacation time there is "Examination Exercises Night." On this night, students recite little speeches and pieces of verse and the like to an audience composed of the influential members of the village government and parents. The boys of the village get their revenge on the schoolmaster on this night. They snatch his wig off after having the sign-painter's son gild the teacher's bald head while he's napping after dinner the day of the exam.

TOM AND HUCK SHARE A SECRET

Tom is still bothered by the secret he shares with Huck concerning Dr. Robinson's murder. He and Huck feel sorry for Potter all the time. For, though Muff Potter's a drunk and a liar, he's never done anything to hurt anybody. The trial begins, and the boys feel even worse. Tom can't stand to see an innocent man hanged. He goes to Potter's lawyer. Finally after much evidence is given by people who recognize Potter's hand in the deed, the lawyer calls Tom Sawyer to the stand. Tom tells all he knows. Before Injun Joe can be arrested, he crashes his way out of the courtroom and flees.

Tom and Huck live in fear that Injun Joe will come back. Tom is happy only during the day. At night he is lonely and full of fear and misery.

But his spirits aren't completely destroyed. As long as it's vacation time, he feels, h twill find some adventure. The best adventure of all, of course, is to dig for treasure. He finds Huck, and the two boys do some digging. They follow the rules set down by some of the novels that Tom's been reading, but they find nothing. Finally they decide to go up to an abandoned ("haunted") house. While they are there, two men come in. The boys drop their tools when they hear the men coming and run upstairs. From where they hide they can hear and see all that the men say and do. One of the men, familiar to the boys as the "deaf and dumb Spaniard" who has been seen in the village the past couple of days, turns out to be Injun Joe.

The men talk about some "big job" they are planning in the village. The younger man feels that it is unsafe to use this old house as a meeting place any longer. Injun Joe agrees with him, but adds that they will need it only a short time. He tells the other to go back up river until he's looked the village over some more-he's got to stay because he wants revenge. Before the two men split up, they dig out their money and take $30 or $40 apiece. Instead of putting the rest of their money back under the hearth where they had hidden it before, they decide to bury it until they pull off their job. Then they can come back to the house and get the money as they head for Texas.

While they're digging the hole to bury the money, they come upon a box full of money that some other gang had hidden many years ago. Then Injun Joe notices that the tools they were digging with had been covered with fresh dirt. They decide it is too dangerous to leave any money in the old house. So they will bury it in Injun Joe's den, "Number Two-under the cross." Just before the two men leave, Injun Joe gets very suspicious because of the tools, and decides to search the house. He is on his way upstairs where the boys are, when the rotten stairway collapses and he falls to the floor. He gives up the search because it is getting dark, and he wants to get his things together before setting out for "Number Two."

Tom is very uncomfortable. He's the only person he can think of that Injun Joe might want to wreak revenge on.

But he isn't so uncomfortable he can't be impressed by all the money he saw. He and Huck set out to find "Number Two." Thinking it's probably a room in one of the taverns, they decide to try all the old keys they can get hold of. But they don't need the keys. Tom tries the door and finds it unlocked. When he opens it, he is surprised to see Injun Joe lying on the floor of the room, drunk and asleep. The boys decide to wait until Injun Joe's out of the room before they try to find the box with the money.

Becky Thatcher comes back to town after a trip to another village (her hometown), and sets a date for the picnic. This distracts Tom's attention from the treasure hunt for a time. The Thatchers charter the ferry boat to take the children to Jackson's Island in the company of a few 18-year-old girls and 23-year-old men. Since the party won't be coming back till late, Mrs. Thatcher tells Becky to stay overnight with someone. But Tom talks Becky out of making plans, because he wants to take her to the Widow Douglas's house. He knows the Widow will have ice cream on hand, and she will be generous with it.

The ferry boat takes the party out to the island, where they eat, then set out to explore the island's main attraction: a large cave. Much later, after dark, the party struggles back to the boat, tired and hungry, and the boat shoves off for the village.

Meanwhile, back in the village, Huck-who has been watching "Number Two" -sees two men coming out. He follows them to the Widow Douglas's house. Just outside the gate, Huck hears Injun Joe plotting to disfigure the Widow because her late husband - the Justice of the Peace - had horsewhipped him and thrown him in jail.

Huck remembers the Widow's kindness to him. He runs to the nearest house in the village, and sends its occupants, the Welshman and his sons, to help her. The next day the village is all full of talk about the excitement at the Widow's house the night before. Then a new subject comes up: Tom Sawyer and Becky Thatcher are missing! The men of the village turn out to search the cave for them. In the meantime Huck gets sick and is delirious with fever at the house of the Welshman, who is good to Huck because he saved the Widow. Since all the doctors are up at the cave searching for Tom and Becky, the Widow comes down to take care of Huck, whose mother is dead, and whose father is the town drunk.

For three days and three nights the villagers search the cave. Except for a hair-ribbon and some markings on the wall, they find no sign of Tom and Becky. Tom and Becky, meanwhile, are wandering in the darkness of the cave, their last candles being all used up. After sleeping a bit, Tom takes a kite string from his pocket, ties it to a rock, and uses it as a line to follow back to his starting point. He explores some side caves, until at one point he sees a hand holding a candle come around a corner. He shouts joyfully, thinking he's been found, until he sees the face that belongs to the hand: Injun Joe! Injun Joe runs away, frightened by the unexpected shout. Tom goes back to Becky, too afraid to do any more exploring. But as time goes on, the hunger he feels makes him a little bit braver, so he starts out again, leaving Becky behind with one end of the string. This time he's luckier. After following two passages to their dead ends, he follows a third until he sees a little speck of daylight. He gropes his way toward it, then sticks his head and shoulders out, and sees the broad Mississippi below him. He goes back for Becky, convinces her he's really found a way out, and gets her out of the cave. They hail a passing boat which takes them to the mainland, and after they've rested, to St. Petersburg. The town goes wild in the middle of the night.

After a couple of days of resting, Tom is told of Injun Joe's attempt to take revenge on the Widow, and of Huck's illness. A couple of weeks later, he learns that Judge Thatcher has had the big door on the cave sheathed in boiler iron and triple locked. He faints when he hears this news. The Judge brings him to and asks him what's wrong. He blurts out: "Oh Judge, Injun Joe's in the cave!"

When the cave door is unlocked, the search party-with Tom and the Judge at its head-finds Injun Joe dead on the ground. He has starved to death. They bury him at the mouth of the cave, and his grave becomes a popular tourist attraction.

By and by Huck gets to feeling better. Tom takes him to the island, where they enter the cave through the hole Tom escaped through. They find the money Injun Joe had, together with guns and moccasins and a leather belt and rubbish. They take the money back to the village, thinking to bury it for safekeeping. Before they get to the woods with it, they are found by the Welshman, who asks them whether they have bricks or old metal in the wagon. They tell him it's old metal. He thinks they mean junk. He insists that they go with him to the Widow's house. When they get there, they discover that the Widow is having a party in honor of the Welshman and his sons because they saved her life.

HUCK TIRES OF CIVILIZATION

The Widow takes the boys upstairs, where she has clean clothes for them, and tells them to wash up and come downstairs when they're ready. Tom's half-brother Sid comes up, and tells the boys that the Welshman wanted them at the party because he was going to surprise everybody by announcing that Huck was the real hero that night. However, Sid continues, it won't be a surprise, not anymore, because everyone knows. Tom cuffs him for ruining the Welshman's surprise out of pure meanness. When he and Huck go down, the festivities begin. Pretty soon the Welshman springs his surprise, which is received with polite but artificial astonishment. Then the Widow says that she's going to adopt Huck, and she gives him some money as a reward for saving her. Tom sees his chance. He hauls out the fortune he and Huck found. It is more money than anyone there has ever seen at one time before, although several people there owned property worth much more than that. Huck is adopted by the Widow. The boy's money is set out at interest. They each get a dollar a day spending money on weekdays, and half-a-dollar on Sundays. This is quite a bit of money for a boy in a small Southern village.

By and by Huck gets tired of civilization, and leaves the Widow's. But Tom gets him to go back by telling him that he is starting a robber gang, and that only respectable people will be allowed in it. Huck promises to go back to the Widow's because he wants to be a robber, and "if I get to be a reg'lar ripper of a robber, and everybody talking 'bout it, I reckon she'll be proud she snaked me in out of the wet."

Comment

Mark Twain indicates in the short preface to this book that the story is primarily an adventure tale for youngsters. It is not, therefore, to be read with the searching criticism of an adult. He indicates that adults may get something out of reading *The Adventures of Tom Sawyer*: an understanding of the life of young people in the small, sleepy villages of the South about thirty years before the Civil War. This is the main attraction of the book. The escapades of Tom Sawyer are no more than the record of the life of a boy in a small town. What does such a boy do for excitement? He makes it up for himself when it isn't already there. He gets a lot of help from the books he's read-books about knights and robbers and famous kings, all of them written from a romantic point of view, all tending to stir up the imagination of an intelligent youngster.

The character of Tom Sawyer is developed pretty much as a model of what we'd consider today to be a "genuine boy." Tom is basically good, but he's by no means the village "Model." Nor does he want to be, although his conscience does bother him from time to time. He's sure he'll go to hell for playing hooky, and lying. He's not overly good. But then, he's not overly bad. He comforts Muff Potter, and testifies in his favor-even though his life is endangered by the testimony. He stands by Becky in the cave and in the schoolhouse when he takes her whipping. He befriends Huck Finn. He condemns Sid's meanness. On the other hand, there is no denying the fact that he's a show-off. He likes to be the center of attraction. And of course, he feeds "Pain-Killer" to the cat, and he does lie, and he does fight with other boys.

In some respect Tom is the carrier of Mark Twain's **satire**. He is portrayed as the product of the kind of reading Mark Twain detested most: the romanticized historical novel. Tom's showiness, his love of the "gaudy," his attempts to make a "big splash," result, as Mark Twain states explicitly in another place, in the kind of courageous man who will unthinkingly cause much sorrow and suffering because he won't recognize a lost cause, or won't do things an easy, realistic way. In other words, he won't be moderate. Such a person overly romanticized the days of knight-errantry, without realistically regarding the hardships and the many perils of medieval life. This is Tom's real failing, not hooky-playing. He fails when he has the opportunity to alleviate Aunt Polly's sorrow, but doesn't. Instead, he lets her (and the entire village) suffer a few more days so that he may return in a "gaudy" manner. The grateful village doesn't mind being made a fool of. But Tom's showmanship is essentially selfish. This is the kind of selfishness stemming from ignorance that Mark Twain saw coming from the type of romantic novel that Sir Walter Scott wrote.

The story itself is very properly called *the Adventures of Tom Sawyer*. It is a loosely unified series of escapades that hangs together mainly because the central character is always the same. There are two plots running through the story at all times, and Tom is the most active character in both of them. The first plot is the love of Tom for Becky. The second includes Tom's quest for treasure and the conflict between Tom and "Injun Joe." Both plots are successfully developed because Tom has a romantic nature, derived as noted above, from his reading. There is very little connection between the two plots other than the fact that the central figure is the same in both.

The plots themselves are developed more or less by coincidental occurrences: for example, Huck's illness after the attack on the Widow's house is a sudden one which the reader has not been properly prepared for. But the illness is necessary in order to develop the suspense which is needed to carry the treasure hunt along. Huck mumbles incoherently about the package the two men were seen to carry out of "Number Two," and he leads us to think it's the treasure. But by and by we find out it was a package of burglar tools. In the meantime we're wondering what became of the money. Huck can't go looking for it, and Tom's lost in the cave. The finding of the money in the cave is a clever twist, but again, it seems gratuitously worked out. No reason is ever given to lead us to think that Tom had the time or interest to look for Injun Joe's "robber den" while he was lost in the cave. The point is, of course, that the story ends "gaudily," as Tom would say, on a note of high adventure and excitement.

In the main *The Adventures of Tom Sawyer* has no moral. It is different from adventure stories children like Tom Sawyer must have read, because it is realistic, not romantic. Tom Sawyer is what he is and does what he does because Mark Twain lived and grew up watching boys in his village do the same kinds of things.

THE ADVENTURES OF TOM SAWYER

TEXTUAL ANALYSIS

CHAPTERS 1-6

CHAPTER I: Y-O-U-U TOM

The first character Mark Twain introduces us to in this novel is the hero's Aunt Polly. As the story opens she is calling for Tom, who doesn't answer. She pulls her spectacles down and looks over them, then puts them up and looks under them - obviously her eyes aren't so bad she needs the spectacles to see through. They are mainly for "style." She continues her search for Tom, but - in Mark Twain's words - "resurrects nothing but the cat." At this crucial moment, while she's calling out the back door again, she hears a noise behind her and turns quickly to catch Tom by the seat of his pants as he's making his getaway from the closet where he's been hiding among the jam jars. Before Polly can warm the seat of his pants with a hickory switch, however, she loses Tom because he pulls an old trick: he tells her to look out behind her, and when she turns her head, he is gone - like a greased flash.

Aunt Polly laughs gently when she realizes that Tom has "put one over on her," but she chides herself nonetheless for not being able to discipline the boy properly. Tom, she thinks to herself, seems to know that she can't punish him except in the heat of the moment. So he has developed a knack for making her laugh or for otherwise postponing the punishment. Her anger can't last because "he's my own dead sister's boy, poor thing, and I ain't got the heart to lash him, somehow." But Polly is a very moral woman, and she realizes she isn't doing right by Tom when she's soft on him. She resolves to be more strict. She knows Tom will have to be punished the next day, which will be Saturday, because he is fairly certainly going to play hooky this afternoon.

At supper Aunt Polly tries to find out for sure whether Tom cut school and went swimming as she suspects. She questions him about how warm it was during the day and tries to catch him in some kind of admission that he went off to the river. But Tom is more clever than she is. He agrees that it has been a very warm day; it has been so warm, in fact, that he and some other boys pumped on their heads to cool off. This is the reason why his hair is still damp.

Although she has lost one round in this battle, Aunt Polly isn't beaten. She asks Tom whether "pumping" required him to undo his shirt collar where she sewed it. Tom proudly opens his jacket and shows her the sewn collar - still intact. Polly tells him to get along on his way. She's sorry she wasn't right, but at the same time she's glad Tom has been a good boy for once. It is at this point that Tom's half-brother, Sid, a good, quiet boy, calls Polly's attention to the fact that Tom's collar is sewn with black thread, whereas Aunt Polly had sewed it with white. Tom doesn't wait to hear Polly's reaction. On his way out the door he says, "Siddy, I'll lick you for that." Off by himself he studies his two needles - one with black and one with white thread - and wishes Polly would choose one or the other color of thread and stick to it.

Mark Twain comments, "He was not the Model Boy of the village. He knew the model boy very well though - and loathed him."

Tom forgets his troubles quickly. He becomes preoccupied with whistling, an accomplishment he's just learned. While strolling along practicing this newly acquired ability, he sees a strange boy, one who is a trifle bigger than himself and quite well dressed for the little village of St. Petersburg. The boys stare at each other and after offering assorted challenges, dares, and insults, fight. Tom wins, but he has to chase the other boy home when the boy hits him with a rock when his back is turned.

When Tom gets home it is late. He climbs in his bedroom window and is met by his aunt, who takes one look at his clothes and decides he will have to be punished the next day, Saturday or no Saturday.

Comment: In describing Tom Sawyer in this chapter Mark Twain sums him up pretty well when he says Tom is "not the Model Boy of the village." Notice how Twain tells us about Tom not by describing his outward features, but by showing how he acts in specific situations. He's clever enough to carry thread to sew up his shirt collar after he goes swimming. He - and this is an important element in Tom's character - is different from "good" boys like Sid and the stranger in that he's straight-forward. He is not a tattle-tale, let alone a sneaky squealer like Sid who pretends to be making an innocent comment while he's obviously "ratting." Nor does he attack people while their backs are turned, like the stranger who heaves a rock at him when his back is turned and then runs home to his mother for protection. And yet, like any normal boy who is to be disciplined, Tom tries to put off his punishment as long as he can, hoping vainly (most likely) that all will be forgotten. He gets into all kinds of trouble - steals jam, plays hooky, goes swimming, and gets in late at night with his clothes all mussed. When he is about to be punished for doing these things, he runs off. But this is normal. Sneaking around is not.

As far as Twain's narrative technique is concerned, notice how he explains the relationship of the characters. Polly tells us that Tom is her nephew, but she tells us this indirectly. Her main point is to chide herself for not being able to discipline Tom. And, of course, the reason for her not being able to do so is a sentimental one, so we not only learn directly that she feels guilty about the way Tom is growing up, but indirectly we learn that he is her nephew (his mother is dead) and that she is a very sentimental sort of person. This indirect way of informing the reader about a character's personality is one of the most important devices in modern realistic fiction. Twain uses it effectively, in this chapter and elsewhere. Notice how Twain tells us that though she is a religious person, she is one of those who does not really know the Bible: "Spare the rod and spoil the child" is not a Biblical aphorism as Polly seems to think. For her it is enough that the aphorism has a kind of Biblical ring to it, and it therefore has all the moral force of the Ten Commandments.

CHAPTER II: WHITEWASHING THE FENCE

The next day, a beautiful Saturday in early summer, finds Tom facing 30 yards of fence with a bucket of whitewash and a long-handled brush. After taking a couple of passes at the fence, he sits down to think of the many things he'd rather be doing than whitewashing a fence. He calls to Jim, the colored boy, who's going to the village well for a pail of water, and tries to convince him to do some whitewashing. But Jim knows better. Aunt Polly has told him to let Tom do the whitewashing. Tom weakens Jim's resolve by promising him a "special" kind of marble - a "white alley" - and by offering to let Jim see his sore toe. While the bandage is being unwrapped, Jim feels a sting and tears off down to the well, his rear burning, and Tom finds himself whitewashing with a will. Aunt Polly walks back to the house with the slipper in her hand.

Tom is unhappy of course. He can think of nothing but the expeditions he's planned for the day. Then he has an inspiration. He picks up his brush and goes to work, peacefully, calmly, carefully, as though he enjoys what he is doing. Soon, his friend Ben Rogers comes skipping along, eating an apple, carefree and happy, pretending he's a Mississippi River steamboat. Tom works along, seeming not to notice Ben's presence until Ben addresses him at least two times. Tom jumps as though, being caught up in work, he's surprised. When Ben begins to tease him about having to work, Tom denies that whitewashing the fence is really work. No boy gets a chance to do this kind of thing every day. Ben stops for a minute and considers Tom's point of view. He watches as Tom maneuvers the brush back and forth, delicately touching up here and there, and in general carrying on as though he is an artist. It's too much for Ben. He asks Tom to let him whitewash for a while. Tom holds off. After all, he tells Ben, Aunt Polly's particular about this fence; she doesn't want just anybody to do it. She wouldn't let Sid or Jim do it.

By this time Ben is eager to work. He offers Tom the core of his apple, and finally the whole apple, for a chance to whitewash. Tom, "with reluctance in his face, but alacrity in his heart," hands Ben the brush. By the time the day is out Tom has amassed a small treasure from the boys of the village, letting them take turns whitewashing the fence. Besides getting this treasure, he has had a pleasant time with plenty of company, and the fence has had three coats of whitewash. The chapter ends with this "moralistic" passage:

If he had been a great and wise philosopher, like the writer of this book, he would now have comprehended that Work consist of whatever a body is obliged to do, and that Play consists of whatever a body is not obliged to do. And this would help him to understand why constructing artificial flowers or performing on a treadmill is work, while rolling tenpins or climbing Mont Blanc is only amusement. There are wealthy gentlemen in England who drive four-horse passenger coaches twenty or thirty miles on a daily line, in the summer, because the privilege costs them considerable money; but if they were offered wages for the service, that would turn it into work and then they would resign.

Comment: This chapter contains what is perhaps the best known incident in American literature: The incident where Tom "sells" work after he decides that he can't buy help. The idea of a clever person turning misfortune into good fortune is an appealing one. But the story is popular for yet another reason: the way Twain develops it.

You will remember that Tom at first tries to buy Jim's help. He almost succeeds, but Aunt Polly ruined the deal. He realizes that he doesn't have enough wealth to buy "even a half-hour" of freedom. It is in this darkest hour, when it seems there's nothing for it but to do the job, that Tom is inspired. Twain does not let us know what Tom's inspiration is, and we are as much puzzled as Ben Rogers is to see Tom working away as though he loves his work. But we know that something is not straight here, which is more than Ben Rogers knows. Although we don't know what's going to happen, the knowledge that something is going to happen amuses us and keeps us eager for the rest of the incident. By developing the incident this way Twain adds a dramatic interest to a story not, after all, that exciting in itself. The paragraph quoted above is characteristic of the satirical essays Twain wrote throughout his career. Note the ironical way in which he refers to himself as "a great and wise philosopher." The tone of the **satire** is kept light this way, in keeping with the story. The intrusion of this odds and ends sort of material into the narrative doesn't destroy the masterly scene it follows, mainly because of the way the aside is written.

CHAPTER III: TOM AS A GENERAL

Tom goes into the dozing Polly to ask if he can go play now that the fence is finished. Polly is surprised. She thought that Tom just taken off long ago, without doing the fence. Her surprise is multiplied when she inspects the fence and finds that the job is well done. She praises Tom, and rewards him with an apple. While she lectures him about how good the apple will taste because he earned it. Tom snitches a doughnut. On his way out of the yard, he meets Sid. He heaves several clods at Sid and hops the fence before Aunt Polly stop him. It is a good feeling, settling with Sid for squealing about the black thread! He meets his friends in the village square where they all play "army." Tom, who is general of one army, outmaneuvers Joe Harper, general of the other.

The New Girl

On his way home he passes Jeff Thatcher's house where he sees a new girl walking in the garden. Before he knows what happens, he forgets his pledges to Amy Lawrence, his girlfriend, and is violently in love with the stranger. He begins to show off - just like a boy - and thinks he is making headway with the girl until she turns to go in the house. He sighs, but is instantly happy again when he sees her throw a pansy over the fence before she disappears into the house. He makes elaborate work of picking the pansy up with his toe so he won't be detected by any of his passing comrades. Hiding around the corner, Tom pins the flower in his jacket next to his heart, "or next to his stomach, possibly, for he was not much posted in anatomy, and not hypercritical, anyway." He hangs around for a while, continuing to show off, hoping the girl is watching him from a window.

Tom is in high spirits when he goes home, and even takes the scolding Aunt Polly gives him for clodding Sid without getting upset. He doesn't mind too much when she raps his knuckles for stealing sugar, even though she doesn't punish Sid for stealing sugar. But when Polly leaves the room for a moment and Sid accidentally breaks the sugar bowl while stealing sugar to show off his immunity from punishment, Tom is all set to see Sid "catch it." He is all excited and ready for the show, when he suddenly feels himself propelled to the floor. Before Aunt Polly belts him again he cries out: "Hold on, now, what'er you belting me for? - Sid broke it!" Realizing her mistake, Aunt Polly wants to console him. But she feels to do so would be a sign of weakness that would be good for discipline, so she keeps quiet and wanders about the house feeling low and troubled. Tom knows she feels this way, but he petulantly will not let on that he knows. Instead, he begins to pity himself, imagining himself dead with Polly crying over him. His imagination is so strong he begins to cry from self-pity. While he's wallowing this way his cousin Mary comes in, fresh, breezy and happy from her week-long visit in the country. Of course, Tom in his present mood can't stand happiness, so he leaves the house and wanders down to the river where he thinks of what a comfort it would be to be drowned. Then he thinks of the new girl. He wonders whether she'd be any nicer to him than the rest of the world has been. Wandering over to her house, he clasps the flower in his hands and crosses his arms over his breast as he lies face up under the window he thinks may be hers. He decides to die there so that she will pity him when she comes out in the morning. But such a happy end is not to be his. A maid opens the window and douses him with a bucket of water. Jumping up angrily, Tom heaves a rock through the window and runs off in the night.

When he gets home he takes off his wet clothes and crawls into bed without saying his prayers. Sid, who shares the room with him, is awake. Seeing the dangerous look in Tom's eyes, he says nothing, but only makes a mental note of the fact that Tom has omitted his prayers.

Comment: Mark Twain develops Tom's character still further in this chapter. Notice how he has Tom make the most of having whitewashed the fence. Tom never tells Aunt Polly he did the work, but he doesn't tell her he did not do the work. He lets her see that the work is done. Just as, earlier, he was quick and proud to let her see the sewn collar, and thus establish his innocence, so now he is advertising his energy and integrity. Tom, like all boys his age, is eager to "score a few points." Mark Twain knew boys well.

Further, when Tom gets rapped for breaking the sugar-bowl, he does pretty much what we would expect him to do: he waits for Aunt Polly to make it up to him. But she doesn't, so he pouts; and by pouting he emphasizes to Aunt Polly the fact that he is really a misunderstood, unloved creature. Of course this is a trick most boys have tried at one time or another, and they usually get the same amount of sympathy that Tom gets: that is, just as much as they can give themselves.

Of course, by having Tom doused by the Thatcher's maid when he reclines under Becky's window (that is the name of the girl Tom has fallen in love with), Twain saves the incident from becoming too maudlin. By injecting this little bit of humor, Twain does more than keep the story from becoming a sentimental "true-story confession." He adds these subtle exaggerations to **burlesque** the typical boy-girl affairs that are so popular in novels.

For all the fact that Tom Sawyer is a simple story about a young boy's adventures, notice how the general **theme** of these three first chapters is that Tom thinks he is unloved and unappreciated. He isn't really, of course. Aunt Polly tells us in Chapter I. But Tom thinks no one loves him. Since most of the adventures in the chapters which follow are going to be based on something Tom does to make people stand in awe of him and to admire him, it is important for Mark Twain to show us, this early in the book, how much Tom needs to be shown that he is loved and wanted.

Notice how Tom spends great time and energy "showing off." Not only when he sees Becky, but also in incidents like those referred to above where he advertises his "goodness" to Aunt Polly, and where he - in self-pity - lies under Becky's window. All of this is showing off, and showing off is an important part to Tom's total personality. Mark Twain develops this element in Tom in a dynamic way. That is, he puts Tom in situations where he will behave like a show off. Twain doesn't just come out and tell us directly that he is burlesquing this part of typical behavior, but he exaggerates so we can't help but know. And, of course, it's much more fun to learn the way Mark Twain teaches than to learn as though from a sermon.

Finally, Twain adds a delicate touch to the character of Sid when he adds the little detail about Sid noticing Tom's omission of prayers. How like a "good" boy, to see the mote in his neighbor's eye but not the beam in his own.

CHAPTER IV: SUNDAY

The next day is Sunday, and all the activities of Aunt Polly's household are directed toward getting ready for church services.

First there is "family worship" at home, which Aunt Polly leads with a prayer and a reading from the Bible. Then Tom must get down to memorizing five verses from the Scriptures, because all children must recite verses at Sunday school. And finally, there is the most cruel ritual of all in Tom's eyes, getting "dressed up" - including putting on shoes, which are never worn during the week - for church. Mary has charge of Tom's memorizing and dressing. By bribing him with a "surenuff" Barlow knife, she gets him to memorize the verses; by leading him outside to the basin, after he's had three chances to do the job himself, and swabbing him down with wash-cloth and soap, she makes him presentable, "a man and a brother...."

At the door of the church, Tom enters into a swapping session with several of his comrades. He trades off some of the treasures he gained at the whitewashing session the day before for the blue, red, and yellow tickets that represent Biblical knowledge. (For every two verses of the Bible he recites, a student receives a blue ticket, for ten blue tickets he receives a red ticket, for ten red ones he receives a yellow. For ten yellow tickets he gets a Bible - a small, cheap Bible, but a Bible presented with great pomp and ceremony in full view of the entire class.)

Mark Twain describes the Sunday school session as being typical of such sessions. There is a great deal of inattention, whispering, bickering, fidgeting and fighting among the students, even among the good students like Sid and Mary.

The class is interrupted by the appearance of visitors: Lawyer Thatcher with an old, feeble man, a "fine, portly, middle-aged gentleman," a lady and a child. Tom recognizes the child: it is the girl he fell in love with the day before. In a moment he is a changed boy. He begins to show-off with vigor; in his happiness he forgets the dousing under the window the night before. The visitors are introduced to the class. The portly gentleman turns out to be the county judge, brother to the local lawyer. Jeff Thatcher, the lawyer's son and one of Tom's comrades, basks in the light of notoriety when he is called up to shake the hand of his distinguished uncle. All in the class envy him to be so close to a man who has traveled all over the county. Even Mr. Walters, the Sunday school superintendent, and the teachers "show off," finding little busy things to do to let the judge know how important they are in their little world. And the Judge, of course, is "showing-off" too, beaming like the great man everyone thinks he is.

Tom Gets A Bible

The only thing lacking to make Mr. Walter's day complete is having someone to give a Bible to. It turns out that only one student has enough tickets - Tom Sawyer. The superintendent is shocked and surprised by Tom's application. He also senses some sort of disaster about to occur. But there is no denying that Tom has the required number of tickets. Tom is moved to the front of the room and given a seat next to the Judge, much to the chagrin of the boys who had traded off their tickets for the wealth Tom got from them the day before. Tom is spellbound with his new splendor and glory. He is so close to the Judge - her father - that he loses his tongue. He manages, after a good deal of prompting, to stammer out his name, but is bound for deeper difficulties. The Judge asks him to show everyone how well he knows the Bible by naming the first two of the Twelve Disciples. Tom, of course, doesn't know the answer. The superintendent can feel the disaster looming:

"Answer the gentleman, Thomas - don't be afraid." Tom still hung fire.

"Now I know you'll tell me," said the lady. "The names of the first two disciples were - "

"David And Goliath!"

Let us draw the curtain of charity over the rest of the scene.

Comment: In this chapter Mark Twain describes and **burlesques** several aspects of what life was like in the little southern village he characterizes in St. Petersburg. In addition, he shows how Tom reacts when he's faced with the opportunity of gaining notoriety or attention. Notice how the first part of the chapter describes Tom's tribulations in getting ready for church. The description could be an exaggerated description of the Sunday mornings of any young boy in early nineteenth century America. The second half of the chapter describes the Sunday school sessions themselves. Notice how Mark Twain uses little details to indicate through **burlesque** that in his opinion these sessions resulted in no benefits of lasting value to either the students or the teachers. No one pays much attention to what's going on - even the "good" children, like Sid and Mary, get involved in the squabbles and talking. And the teachers and superintendent are not capable of controlling the children. They are especially incompetent when the school is visited by an important personage like the County Judge.

In describing the Sunday school group's reaction to the Judge's visit, Twain gives us a scene that explains to some extent why boys like Tom Sawyer were bound to be "show offs." The Judge was respected not because he was a great person, but because he had all the signs of being a great person. He came from a great distance - twelve miles away. He was widely traveled - he had been all over the county. He held an important post which gave him great authority - he was a county judge. To us in the second half of the twentieth century with jet planes and worldwide travel credit cards, the provincial attitude of the villagers is too absurd to be really effective. But the late nineteenth century was only a little different from the early nineteenth century which Twain writes about. The difference was just enough to make the Judge a believable character. To the villagers who could very likely never have needed to go outside their home town in their lifetimes, the Judge represented adventure, novelty and excitement. After all, if you know your village inside out, nothing in it can seem strange and exciting; but anything that happens outside it is bound to seem thrilling and different simply because the setting will be different. The Judge has come from far away and has traveled. The villagers assume some of the excitement and novelty of these faraway places has rubbed off on him. And, because most human beings like adventure, they try to get close to the Judge - to have him notice them - so that he would let some of his glamor rub off on them and also - and this is more important - so that he would not think they are backward simply because they haven't "been around." So they show off. And the Judge, knowing that everyone wants his approval, wants everyone to keep thinking he's a great man. So he shows off too. And everybody in the room is trying to impress everybody else in the room. That's the way people seemed to be to Mark Twain: slightly flawed by a vein of vanity.

Of course, the "curtain of charity" covers Tom's terrible embarrassment. He's tried to show off and has botched the whole job.

CHAPTER V: THE CHURCH SERVICE

Mark Twain describes the church and worshippers in this chapter. Mainly by referring to his mannerisms, Twain describes

Willie Mufferson, the Model Boy of the village whom all the other boys hate. Willie handles his mother as though she is made of cut glass, and he always has a handkerchief - a sure sign of a snob in the eyes of Tom Sawyer and other boys who use shirtsleeves to good advantage.

Twain describes the minister, the way he conducts the services, and the way the congregation -including Tom Sawyer - responds with polite boredom. The only thing that keeps Tom from catching flies and taking them apart during prayer is fear that he'll be "instantly destroyed." The only thing that keeps him from doing this after the prayer is Aunt Polly's watchful eye.

Tom is bored during the long, prosy sermon about how the lion and the lamb shall lie down together on the Day of Judgment. He perks up briefly when the minister tells how they shall be led by a little child. The very conspicuousness of such a position draws Tom's attention, and he wishes he could be that child - providing the lion is tame.

His interest is short-live, however, and he turns to the contents of his pockets to amuse himself. He has a "pinchbug" - a black beetle with large jaws. He plays with it, but when the beetle bites him, he shakes it off, throwing it iron its back in the aisle. A stray dog wandering around inside the church is attracted to it. The dog teases if for a while and is rewarded with a bite on the nose. It yelps and flips the beetle further away, to the amusement of the congregation, which finds these antics more pleasant to contemplate than the picture of hellfire and damnation the preacher is describing for them. The dog wanders about for a few minutes, then returns to the aisle and absent-mindedly sits on the beetle. With a soul-searing howl, it tears around the pews before jumping into the lap of its owner who throws it out the window. It is last seen disappearing across someone's yard. At this point the congregation is hysterical with laughter and trying unsuccessfully to hide its glee behind handkerchiefs and in coughs, grunts and snuffles. The minister, unable to recapture the elevated mood he thought had held the people earlier, brings the sermon to a close.

On his way home, Tom reflects that church isn't so bad when something happens to relieve the monotony. He feels, though, that the dog could have left the "pinch-bug" behind when it escaped from church.

Comment: This chapter contains much description that satirizes small town religious manners and practices. The description is ironical and full of **burlesque** exaggeration. **Irony** is a literary device by which an author expresses something different from (and generally the opposite of) the literal meaning. Now, this chapter seems to be a slightly exaggerated description of how the people in the village dressed and behaved when they attended church, and how the minister conducted services. Twain writes: "And now the minister prayed. A good generous prayer it was and went into details...." He finishes the sentence with a very long list of the people, institutions, and things prayed for. The impression he leaves with us is not so much that the prayer is good, but rather that it is high-flown and bombastic and more of a ritual for its own sake than a sincerely felt prayer.

Notice too how Twain inserts little comments about the people and manners he is describing. These comments make them seem ridiculous. Sometimes the comments seem biting a vicious, as for example the one on politicians: "for they had a mayor there, among other unnecessaries"; or the comment on the habit of reading notices from the pulpit: "a queer custom which is still kept up in America, even in cities, away her in this age of abundant newspapers. Often the less there is to justify a traditional custom, the harder it is to get rid of it."

Tom, you will note, misses the whole point of the Biblical reading about the child leading the lion and the lamb. He thinks only of how grand it would be to be that child standing up before the multitude of all the generations of earth. He feels like showing off, you see.

The last few paragraphs of the chapter are devoted to the "pinch-bug" story. Notice how the incidents in this story, ordinary and not interesting in themselves, become entertaining and humorous when they are cleverly put together by a master storyteller. Part of the success of this story depends on the setting - a dog howling around the city streets is not a necessarily funny sight, and might even be a pitiful one. But a dog howling around inside a church is a funny sight. This kind of dependence on unusual and grotesque connections of elements is characteristic of the broad local humor so popular in the nineteenth and early twentieth centuries. It appeals to the same "funnybone" in us that the picture of the dignified man slipping on a banana skin appeals to. Another important element that makes the story a success is Twain's style. The colorful words and expressions he uses ("vagrant poodle" and the like) all are qualities of the small town storyteller's art. Being concrete they are used to give character to bland and otherwise ordinary occurrences.

The fact remains that the story, as told her, is humorous and entertaining. This is a sign of Mark Twain's talent: he was a master craftsman in humor and **burlesque** who had learned his craft on the American frontier, the birthplace of the rough and ready humor that to this day characterizes American comic art.

CHAPTER VI: SCHOOL

The next morning is Monday, and like all Mondays it is a school day. Tom awakens early, but lies in bed grieving that he has to put himself back under the teacher's surveillance for another week. He almost wishes Saturday and Sunday weren't days off. It's harder for him to go back to school after a weekend than after he's been going for a week. He searches himself for illnesses that could keep him home from school, but except for a loose tooth finds nothing to rejoice about. He doesn't want to tell Aunt Polly about the tooth because she'll just pull it out and he'll have to go to school anyway. He decides he'll give his sore toe a try. Groaning and moaning, he tries to waken Sid. Eventually he has to resort to calling Sid, who gets frightened by the **realism** of Tom's groans. Pretending he's in his last agony, Tom moans to Sid:

"I forgive you everything, Sid. (Groan.) Everything you ever done to me. When I'm gone - ."

Sid rushes to Polly, who - half petrified with fear at the sound of Tom's suffering - nervously asks him what's the matter. Tom answers: "Oh, auntie, my sore toe's mortified!" Aunt Polly is so relieved she half cries and half laughs. Tom knows the toe won't work, so he tells her that, well, the toe seemed mortified - it hurt so he never minded his tooth hurting at all. Polly tells Mary to fetch a piece of silk thread and a hot coal. In panic, Tom gives himself away: he asks her not to pull the tooth - it no longer hurts, he says, and he doesn't want to miss school. Polly pulls the tooth by fastening one end of the string to the tooth and the other end to the bedpost. She then thrusts the burning coal towards Tom's face suddenly. When he jumps out of the way, he leaves his tooth dangling from the bedpost. Tom goes to school. But he has a new toy - the gap in his mouth through which he can spit "in a new and admirable way."

Huckleberry Finn

Before he gets there, however, he meets Huckleberry Finn, the son of the town drunkard. Huck doesn't go to school; he leads a carefree life, unwashed, undisciplined, but also unwanted. Always dressed in cast-off clothes, Huck's ragged appearance is in keeping with his sleeping quarters, an old hogshead in back of the lumberyard and tannery. He is an outcast, and none of the boys in the village is permitted to associate with him.

Tom greets Huck, and asks him what it is he's carrying. Huck replies that it's a dead cat he got from a boy for a blue ticket he got from Ben Rogers and a bladder he got from the slaughter-house. The cat is good for curing warts. Tom and Huck discuss the value of various methods of curing warts. Huck feels that the spunk-water method does not work - he heard this from a Negro who heard it from Ben Rogers who heard it from Jim Hollis who heard it from Johnny Baker who heard it from Jeff Thatcher who was told by Bob Tanner who tried the method without results. Tom replies that Bob Tanner probably stuck his hand in a stump full of rainwater in the daytime and looked at the stump without saying anything. That is a poor way to cure warts, Tom argues. You're supposed to back up to the stump at midnight, "jam your hand in and say: Barley-corn, barley-corn, injun meal shorts, Spunk-water, spunk-water, swaller these warts. and then walk away quick, eleven steps, with your eyes shut, and then turn around three times and walk home without speaking to anybody. Because if you speak the charm's busted."

Huck allows that that is a good way. He describes a technique which involves a bean, and that is another good way. Tom adds an incantation to the method, which he says must be pretty effective because Joe Harper, who has traveled all over (he's been down to Coonville), uses it. Huck then describes the method of using the dead cat. You go to the graveyard about midnight the day a wicked person has been buried. When the devils come to haul him away you throw the dead cat after them with an incantation authorizing the warts to follow the cat which is following the devils to hell. Tom and Huck decide to try the method that night over Hoss Williams' grave. Huck will meow for Tom that night. As the boys part, Tom trades Huck his tooth for a tick Huck picked up in the woods.

Becky

Of course, Tom gets to school late. When he's asked why, he almost lies but stops himself in time when he notices that the only empty seat in the girls' section of the room is next to the new girl, the one he loves. So he admits that he stopped to talk with Huckleberry Finn. For this serious transgression he is whipped and ordered to sit with the girls. This is what he has been hoping for.

He sits next to Becky, who hitches herself away from him a little. When the class's interest in the novelty of Tom's position has worn off, and no one is watching him, Tom gives Becky a peach which she rejects once heartily and a second time faintly before she accepts it. He then arouses her curiosity by drawing a house. He lets her cajole him into showing it to her. Then she asks him to draw a man and herself in front of it. Tom and the girl get to know each other rapidly. She promises to stay at school with him for drawing lessons during the lunch hour. Tom scrawls I Love You on the slate, and after much promising that she won't tell anyone, lets Becky see it. She is pleased, but she blushes and calls him a "bad thing" nonetheless.

At his point the teacher pulls Tom up by his ear and moves him back to his own seat. Tom is happy in spite of this interruption. So happy is he, in fact, that he makes a botch of his lessons, and even loses the spelling medal he had held for several months.

Comment: A great deal happens in this most important chapter. First, Twain describes the kind of home dentistry that was the only dentistry a great many people - even in the twentieth century - ever knew. Notice how this incident develops very naturally out of Tom's very normal reaction to Monday morning - he hates it. The scene is more than a description of do-it-yourself dentistry. It serves as a means of going from one incident to another in the chapter. This business of making transitions is an important part of any novelist's technique.

Two other fairly important incidents occur in this chapter. Both foreshadow the adventures that will make up the largest part of the book. The first of these incidents is Tom's meeting with Huck and their decision to try out the dead cat's wart-removing ability. What they see and how they react is the story of subsequent chapters. Here it will be sufficient to point out that the conversation is a dramatically presented discussion of one of Twain's favorite topics, superstition. Notice that the evidence presented in favor of this or that technique of removing warts is all the most roundabout hearsay, and that the conclusions reached are usually drawn from references to irrelevant authority (such as that Joe Harper ought to know because he's been to Coonville - that having nothing to do with the matter at hand). This is **burlesque** of the reasonableness of folk-religion and superstition.

And, of course, it is here that we meet the very likable ragamuffin, Huck Finn, who is to become not only Tom Sawyer's best buddy and partner in adventure, but also, by becoming the hero of his own adventure story in another novel, is to become

Mark Twain's critical voice speaking out on the many problems that beset humanity. Particular attention paid to Huck Finn and the way Mark Twain describes him in this book will result in a much richer understanding of Huck's character is Huckleberry Finn, a novel much more impressive than Tom Sawyer.

The third incident in this chapter is the one describing Tom's early joyful hour in the seat with Becky Thatcher. The affair as it is described is **burlesque** of typical adult love. Tom stammers, Becky blushes. Tom is daring, Becky reticent. Much more will be said of this affair in the Comment on the next chapter.

THE ADVENTURES OF TOM SAWYER

TEXTUAL ANALYSIS

CHAPTERS 7-11

CHAPTER VII: TOM AND BECKY

To help the time pass until the noon recess, Tom takes out the tick he got from Huck, and begins playing with it. His friend Joe Harper, sitting next to him, joins in the play. They draw a line on the slate and each boy tries to keep the tick from crossing the line. They enjoy themselves until the schoolmaster, who has tiptoed down on them from behind while they are absorbed in the game, belts them. Recess comes at last. Tom tells Becky to give the rest of the girls the slip and double back to the schoolhouse with him. They have the building all to themselves while Tom teaches Becky to draw, blissfully guiding her hand with his. After a short time they get tired of drawing, and fall into conversation. Becky admits she doesn't like rats, not even dead ones to swing around her head on a string; but she does like chewing gum. Tom likes chewing gum almost as much as he likes dead rats, only he doesn't have any gum with him. Becky has some which she offers him on the condition that he give it back. So they take turns chewing the gum for a while, continuing their conversation. They discover that they both like the circus - Tom thinks it's much more fun than church. He tells Becky he's going to be a clown when he grows up. They make lots of money, he says, almost a dollar a day, according to Ben Rogers.

The Engagement

Then with his next breath, he asks Becky whether she's ever been engaged. She answers that she hasn't, so Tom offers to get engaged to her. Before Becky agrees, she wants to know what getting engaged is like. Tom describes it this way:

"Like? Why it ain't like anything. You only just tell a boy you won't ever have anybody but him, ever, ever, ever, and then you kiss and that's all. Anybody can do it."

"Kiss? What do you kiss for?"

"Why, that, you know, is to - well, they always do that."

He cajoles the stammering Becky into letting him whisper that he loves her, and then gets her to say the same to him. After saying the fateful words, Becky jumps up and runs around the classroom, finally hiding - like an ostrich - with her apron over her face. Tom must tug at her and pull her arms down, while he tells her it's all over but the kiss, and that doesn't hurt at all. Finally, she lets him kiss her, and they swear to be true to each other forever. They will choose each other at parties, and walk with each other (when no one else is looking, of course). Things look good, and the future is full of joy for them both until Tom says: "Oh, it's ever so gay! Why, me and Amy Lawrence - " This reference to his old girlfriend tells Becky that she isn't the first girl Tom's been engaged to. The knowledge ruins the whole affair for her. She rejects Tom, taking refuge in tears. She refuses to accept his apologies or understand his explanations or hear his protestations of undying love. She goes so far as to reject his peace-offering, "his chiefest jewel, a brass knob from the top of an andiron." When she strikes it out of his hand onto the floor, Tom walks out, to return to school no more that day. Becky stands waiting for his footsteps to return, but presently becomes aware that Tom isn't coming back. She cries and scolds herself for her hardheartedness, and spends a lonely afternoon surrounded by the rest of the students, none of whom means as much to her as Tom.

Comment: Mark Twain describes young love very effectively here. He includes all the stutterings and stammerings and blushes and secrecy we all know happen the first time a child falls in love. And Becky, young and innocent though she is, is woman enough to take to tears when she learns that Tom has been "engaged" before. She also knows - from some sort of feminine intuition, it appears - that she should be won slowly. Notice the child-like way in which she holds back from getting engaged: she hides her head in her apron so that Tom will have to work to kiss her. This is, on a juvenile level, a typical woman's way of playing "hard to get." Tom, playing the experienced, worldly-wise lover, blunders as men blunder. Here he talks about the good times he's had with another girl.

Notice how Mark Twain develops this picture of youthful friendship. The tone of the scene is almost idyllic. There's no hint of the biting sarcasm and **satire** that Twain uses when he discusses adults. It is this idyllic tone that makes Tom Sawyer so appealing a book to grown-ups who read it and remember the days when they were unscarred by seas of troubles. But the exaggeration in this scene is characteristic of the **burlesque** technique Twain learned in the West. And notice also how Twain keeps Tom's character consistent with what he has made

Tom earlier. Tom is a very literate young man. In his games - as we shall see in the next few chapters - he is bookish; and he tries to live his life by the book too. So, when he's asked why people kiss when they become engaged, he answers. "They all do." That answer become - a logical conclusion from all the stories he's been reading - is evidence enough for Becky. Tom has abstracted an engagement ritual from his reading, and kissing is part of the ritual. Not to kiss would be like baptizing without water. Don't overlook the importance of ritual in Tom's life. Ritual is Tom's play life. Things must be done with proper respect for their form, and he carries this ritualism over into his love affair.

CHAPTER VIII: TOM DAYDREAMS

On leaving the school, Tom runs for half an hour, dodging the lanes his comrades would be using to return from lunch, until he arrives at a dense wood behind the Widow Douglas' mansion. He goes to the center of the wood, which he knows extremely well, and there sits on the moss under an oak. He is hurt and angry and melancholy; he sits a long time, wishing he were dead like Jimmie Hodges. Becky will be sorry someday, he thinks: someday when it's too late. He wishes he could die - temporarily.

His daydreams turn to ways in which he can "show them all." Maybe he'll become an Indian chief, return to the village dressed in all his regalia and break up Sunday school with a blood-curdling war whoop. Or, better still, he'll be a pirate with a black ship named Spirit of the Storm. Then he'll return to the village in all his criminal splendor to hear the admiring voices whisper, "It's Tom Sawyer the Pirate! - the Black Avenger of the Spanish Main!"

Now that he's decided to run away from home the next morning and get started on his piratical career, he sets about gathering his belongings. He digs under a rotten log nearby until he hits a hollow "treasure house." Laying his hand on the roof of the shapely little house, he mutters an incantation, pulls the house out of the ground, opens it and is astonished to find only one marble. Peeved because he had done everything he should have done to get back all the marbles he's ever lost, he tosses the single marble away. He concludes that his charm didn't work because somebody "witched" him. To test this conclusion, he calls on the doodle-bug to tell him why he didn't get his marbles back. When the doodle-bug simply darts in and out of its hole, Tom is satisfied; obviously the bug is afraid to say anything because a witch has had a hand in Tom's disappointment. Rather than quarrel with a witch, Tom gives up the quest for his lost marbles. He finds - with the aid of another incantation - the marble he has just thrown away. At this moment he hears a trumpet blast (from a toy trumpet, of course) in the woods.

Tom And Joe Harper Play Robin Hood

He quickly strips off his jacket and trousers and arms himself with a bow and arrow, a wooden sword and a tin trumpet he had hidden behind another rotten log. He is now Robin Hood; his shirt tail hanging down around his untrousered legs is to all intents and purposes a medieval gown. Blowing an answering blast through his trumpet, he gives orders to his imaginary merry men and accosts Joe Harper (Guy of Guisborne) who approaches through the brush. The two boys play at Robin Hood for some time, Tom prompting Joe who doesn't have all his lines memorized. They fence with the wooden lath swords, taking turns being hero and villain, winner and dead man. By and by Robin Hood gets killed treacherously, and a whole band of "weeping outlaws" (Joe) takes him off to a burying ground. The scene is touching but ruined when Tom lights unexpectedly on a nettle and jumps up a little too lively to be a believable dead man. With the game ended, the boys get dressed for home, hide their weapons and grieve that the days of outlaws are gone. "They said they would rather be outlaws a year in Sherwood Forest than President of the United States forever."

Comment: Notice how resourceful Tom is. He can bounce back after troubles and disappointments with no real emotional scars. He forgets his problems in the pleasant occupations of the moment and is ready to get his satisfactions by imagining himself to be what he wishes he could be. There is never any reason to expect Tom to seriously undertake running away from home to learn the pirate's trade: not while his first thought is to collect his marbles before he goes.

Notice, too, that Tom doesn't think of coming back from his piracies to destroy the village. He only wants to stroll up and down the streets in his gaudy black and red regalia and be wondered at. There's no problem of deep seated hostility here; it's all play.

The way Twain develops this play or "little boy" aspect of Tom is interesting. He uses such devices as having Tom play by the book, but misunderstand the meaning behind the book. While he and Joe are fencing, Joe insists that Tom should pretend he's killed. Tom answers: "I can't fall; that ain't the way it is in the book. The book says, 'then with one backhanded stroke he slew poor Guy of Guisborne.' You're to turn around and let me hit you in the back."

There is a big difference between a backhanded stroke and hitting a man in the back. The fact that Tom doesn't seem to be aware of this difference leads us to suspect that he doesn't really understand the whole world of piracy, robbery, murder and rape he so eagerly wishes he inhabited. This is going to be important when Tom does eventually come face to face with the criminal world.

CHAPTER IX: A SOLEMN SITUATION

That night, sometime after Sid falls asleep, Tom hears Huck's "meow." He climbs out the window and joins Huck, who is waiting there with his dead cat. They go to the dismal graveyard, scary with the rounded boards leaning this way and that in place of tombstones over the unkempt graves. They find Hoss Williams' grave and hide themselves in a grove of willows a short distance away to wait for the devils who are coming at midnight for the dead man's soul. By and by the boys hear a noise and see a light coming towards them. Thinking the light is "devilfire," they regret that they've come out. Huck asks Tom to pray; the only prayer Tom can think of in this moment of crisis is "Now I lay me down to sleep." Suddenly Huck shushes Tom when he recognizes the voices coming towards them: one of them belongs to Muff Potter, a ne'er do well in the village. Tom recognizes the second voice as belonging to Injun Joe, a "murderin' half-breed." The third voice belongs to young Doctor Robinson, a respected physician. The three men have come to steal Hoss Williams' corpse so Dr. Robinson can use it for scientific purposes.

Injun Joe and Muff Potter dig up the corpse. There is an argument between them and the doctor when they demand more money than they had agreed upon to do the job. The argument ends with Joe reminding the doctor he has a grudge against him for causing Joe's arrest for vagrancy five years earlier. Joe threatens the doctor with his fist. When the doctor knocks Joe down, Muff joins the fight, dropping his knife to wrestle with the doctor. Robinson lays Muff out with the headboard from one of the graves, but is stabbed by Injun Joe who has picked up Muff's knife. At this point, Tom and Huck have seen enough. At sight of the murder, with the principals' attention diverted, Tom and Huck run for their lives.

Joe isn't even aware that the boys were ever there. He is busy robbing the doctor's body and putting the knife in Muff's hand. A few minutes later Muff comes to, and Joe tells him that it was bad business for Muff to have killed the young doctor. Muff, his mind besotted with drink and clouded by the blow on the head, is an easy victim. He believes he killed Robinson and begs Joe not to squeal. Joe promises, and the two men part. While Muff is running away, Joe examines the scene of the murder, and mutters that Muff will not remember he left his knife behind until he's gone quite a distance. By then he'll be afraid to come back to the graveyard for it.

Comment: At last Tom is meeting real adventure. He and Huck witness real grave robbery and a real murder. They run away in fear for their lives, a normal reaction for boys. See how careful Twain is to let us know that the "fearless" Avenger of the Spanish Main is a boy at heart? Tom is so afraid - and Huck is, too - that even before anything foul happens, when the voices, lights and figures approaching through the cemetery might be the very devils he came looking for, he forgets his prayers in his fear.

Compare Tom's reaction to the murder of the doctor with his reaction to the murder of bold Robin Hood in his play. Notice the significantly different way in which Tom behaves in his game life and in real life.

CHAPTER X: THE SOLEMN OATH

The two boys, meanwhile, are still running. They run on and on, without stopping, until they get to the old tannery, where they drop to the floor exhausted, their pulses beating wildly. After they've calmed down somewhat, they discuss the significance of the events they've just witnessed. Huck reckons that if

Doctor Robinson dies, "hanging'll come of it." In answer to Tom's question whether they should tell anyone what they saw, Huck replies:

"What are you talking about? S'pose something happened and Injun Joe didn't hang? Why he'd kill us some time or other, just as dead sure as we're a-laying here."

It is obvious to the boys that Muff Potter won't tell on Joe: Muff was unconscious at the moment of the murder and so won't know who killed Robinson. They decide to "keep mum." Huck suggests that they swear in blood to a written oath; anything less, like holding hands and promising never to tell-as Tom suggests-would suffice for promising things to girls. But this secret is serious, life and death, man business. Tom agrees with Huck. On an old piece of wood, he writes out this oath:

"Huck Finn and Tom Sawyer swears they will keep mum about this and they wish they may drop down dead in their tracks if they ever tell and Rot."

Tom draws blood from his thumb with one of his needles and signs. Then he teaches Huck how to make an "H" and an "F." While they are burying the shingle with proper ritual, they do not see the figure creeping into the other end of the ruined building. They continue to whisper together about how breaking the oath any circumstances will cause them to drop dead, when their conversation is suddenly interrupted by the baying of a dog outside, not ten feet from them. Their fears that it is a stray dog are realized when Tom gets up enough nerve to look through a crack in the wall and identify the animal. The boys snuffle and cry, wishing they had lived better lives. Huck cries because he's sure he'll go to hell, since he's never had the chances the other boys in the village have had. He's stolen and smoked, and he's never been to Sunday School. Tom looks out at the animal again and notices that it has its back to them. This relieves them of their immediate fear. But they become aware of strange noises coming from the other end of the building. They investigate the noise, discovering Muff Potter snoring in a drunken sleep. The dog is facing in his direction, baying with its nose pointing to heaven. This is a sure sign that Potter will die. The boys separate after discussing whether the superstition is true or false, and concluding that Potter is a "goner."

Tom goes home and to bed. Next morning he oversleeps - Sid has apparently told Aunt Polly how late Tom was out - because no one rouses him out of bed. Tom feels low and mean after breakfast when Aunt Polly lectures him and cries over him. When he gets to school, he is whipped - along with Joe Harper - for playing hooky the day before. His heart is finally shattered when he discovers the brass andiron knob, returned by Becky. This is the ultimate rejection.

Comment: Notice what a large part superstition plays in this chapter. This subject is one of Mark Twain's favorite themes. He points out how the evidence for superstition rests largely upon subjective observations and conjectures made by irresponsible authorities. But, and this is important, the evidence is always fairly concrete, and it is this concreteness that convinces people like Huck of the soundness of superstitious beliefs.

Notice too that in this chapter we are beginning to see a real difference between Tom and Huck. It is Huck who very practically points out that they had better keep quiet about what they saw. And when they decide to seal their lips with an oath, it is Huck who very practically calls for the most binding oath that can be had. Huck's suggestions are made from an awareness of their dangers; Tom's book-learning may provide the ritual that's required, but Huck has to see a need for that ritual in terms of the immediate situation in which he finds himself.

CHAPTER XI: MUFF POTTER COMES HIMSELF

When word of the murder gets to the village about noon that day, even classes are dismissed as the villagers flock to the graveyard to view the scene of the grisly crime. Tom and Huck meet there, but look away from each other, afraid that someone will see the knowledge in the glances that pass between them. Because Muff Potter's knife has been identified, the villagers conclude automatically that Muff did the killing. Injun Joe faces Muff, who comes on the scene and is arrested, and lies about the murder. Tom and Huck, hearing the lies, wait for lightning to strike Joe. When nothing happens to him, either then or at the inquest when he repeats his lies under oath, the boys conclude he is under the potent protection of the devil, so they strengthen their resolves to not tell what they have seen. No sense getting the devil mad at you, they figure. Potter, meanwhile, sobs out that he is innocent.

The villagers, with Injun Joe's help, lift Dr. Robinson's body into a wagon to take it into town. Blood oozes from the knife wound as the body is lifted. Huck and Tom hope someone will notice this and connect the oozing blood with Injun Joe's presence. Instead, one of the crowd cries out that the body was less than three feet from Muff Potter when it bled. Obviously Muff murdered the doctor.

Tom's Conscience

For a week Tom's conscience bothers him and disturbs his sleep so noticeably that one morning at breakfast Sid comments on

Tom's restlessness. Aunt Polly, worried at first, finally attributes the horrible fear in Tom's nocturnal shoutings to the murder; the horrible killing causes even her to have nightmares, she says. Tom, however, takes care to bandage up his jaw every night from now on, under pretence of having a toothache.

Moreover, Tom's conscience bothers him too much. He is so disturbed that he does not join in the mock inquests his comrades hold on dead cats in imitation of the real one they saw at the graveyard. Sid notes that Tom lacks interest in these proceedings, never acting as either coroner or witness. This is behavior quite contrary to what one expects of Tom. But every day or two, Tom goes to the little jail that holds Muff, and gives Muff little comforts such as he can get hold of. This eases his conscience somewhat.

In the meantime, a few of the villagers have spoken of tarring and feathering Injun Joe for body-snatching, but no one can be found who is willing to antagonize Joe by leading the party. Things are forgotten for a while.

Comment: Notice in this chapter how Twain depicts the miscarriage of justice. Whose responsibility is it? Why, that of the very people justice is supposed to protect. It is they who, eager to jail Muff on circumstantial evidence, do not consider the source of the testimony against him. They all know that Injun Joe is a liar, and they all know he was body-snatching, same as Muff, but they don't question the veracity of his statements. The scene, if it weren't so tragic, would be a powerfully written **burlesque** on justice in a democracy.

Notice too how Mark Twain uses superstition in this chapter. There is an old superstition that the body of a murdered man will bleed in the presence of the murderer. Notice how the villagers interpret the ooze from Robinson's body to mean what they would like it to mean. Strictly speaking, any of the villagers present in the graveyard could be the murderer, especially those who are handling the body when the blood starts to ooze. Huck has a chance to see superstition in action now. Is it any wonder he believes in very few superstitions, and those only when he's seen practical evidence of their workings?

The question of whether God takes a hand in man's affairs is settled-for Tom and Huck, at least - by the fact that no lightning comes from heaven to strike Injun Joe dead for his perjury.

Notice how Tom tries to salve his conscience by taking little comforts like tobacco to Muff in the jailhouse. His behavior in this respect is very much like that of the typical good boy who visits prisoners. (The typical good boy might visit the prisoner with Bible tracts rather than tobacco, of course, but that really isn't important here.) We shall see in a later chapter how Muff reacts to this interest of Tom's, which he doesn't know is fairly selfish since Tom is getting something out of his trips to the jailhouse: he's trying to ease his conscience.

THE ADVENTURES OF TOM SAWYER

TEXTUAL ANALYSIS

CHAPTERS 12-21

| CHAPTER XII: TOM SHOWS HIS GENEROSITY

Tom's mind drifts away from its preoccupation with murder because Becky Thatcher is sick and has stopped coming to school. He worries about her so much that life is no longer joyful. His moodiness and lack of "spirit" scare Aunt Polly, who is a victim of the health faddists and quacks, into giving him treatments and medicines designed to pep him up. One of these preparations, "Painkiller," is particularly abominable. She doses Tom with it until he feels the only way to make her stop giving it to him is to ask for it several times a day. Unfortunately, Polly takes this for a sign that the medicine is working, and is only too happy to let Tom have all he wants. As a result, Tom begins dosing a crack in the floor with it. One day, Peter, Polly's cat, happens along while Tom is giving the floor its daily dose. The inevitable happens. Peter gets the medicine. (He is so happy to get it, Twain tells us, Tom has to pry his mouth open.) The cat is instantly "energized." It tears the room apart while doing somersaults and handstands, and is just ready to fly out the window with the flower spots when Polly comes in to find out why Tom is rolling on the floor laughing himself silly. Polly notices the spoon and medicine, and asks Tom why he would be so mean as to pour that medicine into the poor, dumb animal. Tom replies:

"I done it out of pity for him - because he hadn't any aunt."

"Hadn't any aunt! - you numbskull. What has that got to do with it?

"Heaps. Because if he'd a had one she'd a burnt him out herself! She'd a roasted his bowels out of him 'thout any more feeling than if he was a human."

Aunt Polly takes Tom off the medicine. He gets to school this day and sees Becky. In an excess of joy, he begins prancing around and "showing off" to get her attention, but is crushed when she says, loudly enough for him to hear, "Mf! some people think they're mighty smart - always showing off!"

Comment: This chapter serves several purposes. It serves first, as relief to keep the emotional intensity of the chapters dealing with the murder from getting too overwhelming. Remember, while the book contains a great deal of horror, it is basically a humorous children's book.

It serves also to build suspense in the murder story by holding up the development of that plot. It takes us back into the love story which, as we shall see, is going to get tied in with the murder story. By being able to alternate these two plots, Twain is able to vary the pace of Tom's adventures and keep them from becoming a set of disjointed incidents.

Finally, the chapter focuses our attention on Tom as the center of the novel, and therefore the character who provides unity in the structural framework of the adventures. Notice how Tom seems to have a series of ups and downs. Twain seems to be working out the tale almost the way a composer works out a piece of music: slowly building it up to a **climax** which clears the air and releases emotion in a great surge. To build the emotion up slowly so that it won't spend itself in a premature **climax** that is not really satisfying. Twain adds to the emotion a little at a time, in this series of "ups and downs." These are reflected in the happiness Tom feels in this chapter when he gets to school after the "Painkiller" **episode**, his sadness when he learns Becky isn't there, and again in his joy when he sees her, and in his embarrassment when she "cuts" him.

CHAPTER XIII: THE YOUNG PIRATES

Tom plays hooky after the rebuff by Becky. He wanders around in the woods, feeling sorry for himself, and thinking he'll run away from home and be a pirate. At this point he meets Joe Harper, whose feelings are the same as his own: Joe's mother whipped him for drinking some cream he didn't even know about. The two boys decide to run away together and be pirates on Jackson's Island, a long wooded island that lies about three miles below St. Petersburg, where the Mississippi is about a mile wide. They find Huck Finn and get him to join them. Then they separate for a while, going about to all their friends, hinting that something big and mysterious is about to happen.

The three boys meet again about midnight, laden with provisions - hams and bacon, fish lines and all the assorted gear they'll need for living in the woods of the uninhabited island. Tom, as the "Black Avenger of the Spanish Main," commands the loading and sailing of the raft they have "captured." He gives orders like a professional to Joe Harper (the "Terror of the Seas") and Huck ("The Red Handed") Finn. It's about two in the morning when the raft lands at the sandbar about two hundred yards from the head of the island. The boys unload it, cache their provisions, and have a hefty meal of bacon and corn pone before stretching out on the grass to contentedly discuss their new situation while Huck carves out a corn-cob pipe and lights up. Huck is dismayed when the talk turns to uniforms and regalia. He isn't wealthy and can't afford diamonds and gaudy clothes. But Tom and Joe encourage him, telling him that things will be better after they have had a few adventures. Huck drifts calmly off to sleep, while Tom and Joe say their prayers to themselves and fight their consciences because they've stolen real food - hams and bacon - which is sinful and not at all like snitching doughnuts or apples. Inwardly, each resolves never again to let his piracy "be sullied with the crime of stealing."

Comment: In this chapter Mark Twain gives us a lively and interesting description of adventure, Tom Sawyer style. The very idea of living in the woods on one's own with no restriction is appealing to a young boy, and Mark Twain knows how to play on this appeal so as to make the incident almost idyllic in innocence. There is a great deal in this (and the next) chapter which foreshadows the great river journey of Huck Finn in Twain's next novel of boyhood.

Notice how Huck agrees to join the pirate gang because all careers are the same to him. He is free and unfettered so he sees the similarity of most occupations and the similarity of their aims. Note that he is the only pirate that sleeps soundly, unencumbered by a conventional conscience that bothers him for stealing. This conscience trouble that Tom and Joe have is a clue to the conflict each of the boys will face before the adventure is over.

CHAPTER XIV: CAMP LIFE

Next morning the boys awaken, refreshed and eager to begin their adventures. They romp and swim and eat and generally enjoy themselves, pushing out of their minds the little pangs of homesickness they are beginning to feel. Presently they hear a curious sound. It is the village ferryboat firing its cannon over the water. This is done whenever someone drowns. The theory is that the noise of the cannon will make the body rise to the surface so it can be brought ashore and buried. It suddenly dawns on Tom that the people on the ferryboat are looking for him, Joe, and Huck. The boys realize that they are now the talk of the town - people are regretting having been mean and unkind to them; all other boys are envying them. This is great!

The boat searches all day and finally goes back in for the night. The boys discuss the pleasure they feel in their new notoriety. By and by it occurs to them that some people in the village aren't having so good a time this night. The grief of relatives and families is real. When Joe puts out a "feeler" about going back home, Tom and Huck wither him with scorn. But after Huck and Joe fall asleep, Tom writes two notes on pieces of bark. One of these he leaves with Joe and Huck, together with some of his treasures; the other he puts in his jacket pocket before he cautiously creeps away from the camp and heads toward the sandbar.

Comment: This chapter continues the idyllic description begun in Chapter XIII, and develops the plot of one of Tom's "play" adventures. By inserting here two statements that the boys are slightly homesick, Twain prepares us for the rest of the adventure. Tom is beginning to see an opportunity for some notoriety in this adventure. Notice how quick he is to deride Joe's hint that they all go home, and notice how secretive he is about leaving the camp; he waits until the others are asleep before he creeps away.

The village steamboat will be called on to fire over the water again in Twain's next novel, *The Adventures of Huckleberry Finn*. There are many instances of Twain's using details over and over in his writing. In this case the repetition occurs because the detail is a real one drawn from Twain's own boyhood on the Mississippi. There is, of course, no basis in fact for the activity; corpses do not rise to the surface just because a cannon is fired over the water. The repetitive use of details in several places in his writing afforded Mark Twain an opportunity to develop his narrative skills.

CHAPTER XV: TOM RECONNOITERS

Tom swims to the Illinois shore where he "hitches" a ride to St. Petersburg on the Missouri shore in the yawl that is trailed behind the ferryboat. He goes to Aunt Polly's house and looks through a lighted window where he sees Polly, Mary, Sid and Joe Harper's mother gathered in a corner of the room by the bed, with the bed between them and the door. He goes to the door and opens it just enough to allow himself to creep through on his hands and knees. When Polly sees the candle blowing she sends Sid to close the door. Tom barely makes it under the bed. He lies there listening to the women grieve over their lost boys, and hears Polly lecture Sid who dares to "hope Tom's better off where he is" but rather doubts it. Tom learns that people think the boys drowned while making a trip by raft to the next village below St. Petersburg. This is Wednesday night. If the bodies aren't found by Sunday the searchers will give up hope, and the boys' funerals will be held during regular church services.

Mrs. Harper eventually goes home, and Sid and Mary go to their rooms. Polly kneels down and prays for Tom. All that he hears makes Tom want to jump out and tell Polly he's safe. But he restrains himself. He waits till she's asleep, then he debates with himself, finally deciding not to leave the note he has written. Instead, he kisses Polly and leaves.

He takes the skiff from the ferryboat and crosses to the Illinois shore. There he leaves the skiff at the ferry landing and walks along the shore till he's abreast of the island. After a short nap he swims back to the island, and enters camp at breakfast time, just as the other boys are about to divide up the treasures he left with the note telling them to keep the goods if he's not back before breakfast.

After the meal, Tom narrates - with some exaggeration - his adventures. The boys feel proud of what they've done. Huck and Joe go fishing and exploring, while Tom hides away for some well-deserved sleep.

Comment: See the Comment to Chapter XVI.

CHAPTER XVI: A DAY'S AMUSEMENTS

After supper on Thursday, the boys hunt up some turtle eggs, which they feast on before going to sleep and again at breakfast Friday morning. They spend Friday swimming and wrestling and playing marbles, but after a while become depressed as their feelings of homesickness return to settle over them with doubled intensity. Joe decides to go home. Huck says he will join Joe. Tom, as down in the dumps as they, wants to go with them, but because he has a secret plan, also wants to stay. He tries to convince the other two to stay with him, but no arguments will prevail. When Huck and Joe are halfway to the sand bar, Tom rushes out to them and tells his "secret" plan. The two would-be deserters turn back joyfully. If he had told them at the very beginning, they say, they would never have started to leave, but Tom knows better. He makes up an excuse for not having told them, but he really had been afraid the secret wouldn't hold them long. So he held it as a "last seduction."

That afternoon Huck teaches Joe and Tom how to smoke. The two novices boast of how easy and pleasant smoking is, and of how they'll impress the other boys with their skill when they go back to school. By and by Joe remembers he's lost his knife; Tom offers to help him find it. Sometime later, Huck finds both boys pale and asleep in the woods: "something informed him that if they had had any trouble they had got rid of it." At supper that night Tom and Joe turn down Huck's offer of tobacco.

About midnight Joe wakes up the other boys: a bad storm is brewing and they will be caught in it. Lightning begins to flash, and a strong wind comes up, and then comes the rain, in scattered big drops at first, settling to a heavy drenching rain. The boys run through the woods on the island looking for shelter as the lightning topples trees around them. In Twain's words" "It was a wild night for homeless young lads to be out in." But the storm finally lets up and stops, and the boys return to camp wonderstruck at the powers they saw displayed. The tree under which they had made their beds is destroyed, and their fire-except for a little spot on the bottom side of the reflecting log they had built it against-is washed out. They nurse the sparks back to brightness and raise their fire again by feeding it dry chips and bark from the undersides of fallen logs. Now they dry off their ham and have another feast until morning, because there isn't a dry spot they can sleep in.

The next day, Saturday, Tom sees the signs of homesickness coming over Joe and Huck again. He gets up a game of Indians and settlers which turns into a game of three hostile Indian tribes attacking one another. They kill each other off by the scores. A good, gory day it is.

About supper time they gather in the camp, but feel that hostile tribes cannot eat together without first smoking the pipe of peace. Tom and Joe cautiously take whiffs off Huck's pipe. To their amazement, they don't get sick. So they smoke another pipe after supper, bragging and boasting of their success. They don't have to go look for a knife this time.

Comment: In these two chapters, Mark Twain is developing the plot of the **episode** that brings Tom, Joe and Huck the kind of notoriety and conspicuousness Tom admires most and is always on the watch for. In Chapter XV, Tom sneaks back to Aunt Polly's house with a note that says he and Joe and Huck are safe. Notice how Tom decides not to leave the note when he learns of the funeral plans. He is an opportunist in this regard. (Mark Twain maintains reader interest by not having Tom decide to keep the note until well after he overhears the talk. By thus postponing Tom's decision, Twain manages to keep from divulging Tom's secret-which we won't learn until the next chapter.) This kind of opportunism and impulsiveness is one of Tom Sawyer's major personality traits and marks him as a boy, not a man.

The **episode** is further developed through the "ups and downs" Tom has when he gets back to the island and finds he must struggle to keep the gang together. Twain effectively uses the boys' homesickness throughout Chapter XVI to build toward the **climax** which is going to come in Chapter XVII. He stretches the suspense by interrupting the narrative with the storm and smoking **episodes** which themselves lend drama and humor to the private adventure. The suspense is heightened by the fact that although Tom tells the boys his secret, Twain does not tell it to us. This skillful manipulation of several dramatic, humorous and descriptive elements to lend verisimilitude to and to heighten the narrative suspense of an **episode** is characteristic of Twain's keenly developed narrative technique.

Note the descriptive passages of life on the river. By using concrete "boy" words and phrases, Twain builds a description of nature that does not sound as bookish as most descriptions of this sort found in nineteenth century fiction and travel writing. This same kind of description, more highly developed, is found in *Huckleberry Finn*.

CHAPTER XVII: MEMORIES OF THE LOST HEROES

Saturday is no happy day in the village. Everyone wanders about absentmindedly. The children have no interest in their games; they can only talk quietly about their memories of the lost boys. Some boys brag that they were beaten up by Tom Sawyer, others that they were tricked by him. Becky wishes she had Tom's brass andiron knob again.

When the Sunday School is finished the next morning, the villager gather in the church for the funeral services. While the clergyman is eulogizing the boys, the church door creaks open and the three "dead" boys come marching up the aisle. There is great joy in St. Petersburg that day. Even Huck comes in for Aunt Polly's loving attention, as the congregation bursts out with "Praise God from Whom All Blessings Flow." While Tom stands there feeling the proudest he's ever felt in his life, there are those among his elders who feel they wouldn't mind being "sold" like that again if they could hear "Old Hundred" sung with such deep sincerity every time.

Comment: So that is Tom's great secret: to come back from the dead on the day of his funeral. He has attained one of his boyish dreams, to die temporarily, and let everyone realize how important he is to them. One of the secrets of this novel's success is that it offers each of us a means of vicariously experiencing some of the childish dreams we've all had.

Note that Twain does not **burlesque** the funeral or the events immediately following it. Indeed, the tone in which he describes the singing of "Old Hundred" seems to carry admiration for these people who, sorry specimens of humanity though they often are, deeply feel and express gratitude for the safe return of the boys they thought were dead. Mark Twain doesn't blast away satirically and sarcastically at everything people do. He is careful to satirize and **burlesque** only those things that merit his condemnation.

From the point of view of technique, note how Twain draws the **episode** to a rapid conclusion after the **climax**. He takes great pains in the first two pages of this short chapter to give us a clear impression of the villagers' feelings-sincere feelings they are. Then he breaks the bubble of suspense rapidly: the boys troop into church and the mood of the congregation is suddenly changed from sadness to joy. After a brief description of the singing of the hymn of thanksgiving, the **episode** is drawn to a rapid close.

CHAPTER XVIII: THE HERO

Mary and Polly treat Tom lovingly Monday morning at breakfast. But Polly mentions that if Tom loved her at all, he would have come back and left some indication that he was not dead, only run away. Mary defends Tom, saying he's not mean, only thoughtlessly impulsive. To make Polly feel better, Tom recounts the events he observed the night he came over from the island, saying that he dreamed them. Polly gets excited. She's always known that dreams are meaningful, and she's going to go right over to Joe Harper's mother - who doesn't believe in dreams - and tell her about this. She is overjoyed that Tom thought of her suffering. Sid injects, "It was very kind, even though it was only a-dream." Polly shuts him up, sends the children off to school, and heads for Mrs. Harper's.

At school, Tom and Joe are heroes. Basking in notoriety, they swagger and describe their adventures with boyish exaggeration, then completely stun the other children by lighting up their pipes. Tom decides that he can live on glory. He doesn't need Becky who is showing off now, trying to catch his attention the way he tried to catch hers before he ran away. She notices how he has been talking more to Amy Lawrence than to any other girl. In final desperation she says to one of her friends - loud enough for Tom to hear - that she's going to have a picnic when school lets out, and anyone can come whom she invites. Tom knows this is a peace offering, but rejects it, continuing his narration to Amy of his adventures on the island. Becky is dispirited when Tom doesn't, like all the others, ask if he can come to the picnic too. She hides away for a while, having a good cry. Then she decides to take vengeance. At recess she lets Tom find her with Alfred Temple, a boy from St. Louis with the typical St. Louis snobbishness Tom hates. When Tom sees the two together, their heads close over a book, he is filled with anguish. He finds an excuse to get rid of Amy and spends the rest of the recess pretending he is beating Alfred to a pulp.

At noon he goes home, leaving Becky at school with Alfred. When Becky notices that Tom isn't there to suffer at the sight of her and Alfred, she realizes that she has driven Tom away. On the verge of tears, she wishes she hadn't overdone things so, and when Alfred interrupts her moody silence she chases him away. Alfred realizes he has been used to make Tom jealous. Peevishly, he gets even with Tom by pouring ink on Tom's spelling book where the teacher will be sure to see it. Becky, who happens to look in the classroom window, sees what Alfred is doing. She is torn between the desire to find Tom and tell him and the desire to punish him for slighting her that morning. She decides to punish Tom by letting him take the whipping he'll surely get for having ink on his book.

Comment: This chapter continues the **burlesque** of the affair. Notice how well Mark Twain makes these children and their ways reflect adult behavior, emotions and motivations. The children seem to be quite good at stumbling on effective ways to make each other miserable. In the opening scene of this chapter Tom is described this way: "'Now, auntie, that ain't any harm,' pleaded Mary; 'it's only Tom's giddy way-he is always in such a rush that he never thinks of anything.'" Moments later Tom shows how well Mary knows him by telling Polly about his wonderful "dream."

Notice, though, that Tom's purpose in lying is not to get famous or to cause trouble, but to make Polly feel good. Polly is going to go tell Mrs. Harper about the dream. And here she is in such a rush it never occurs to her, as it does to Sid, that the dream is too perfect in all its details to be a dream. Nor does she take the responsibility for her embarrassment when she learns from Mrs. Harper that Tom really did come to the village. Instead, she scolds Tom for letting her make a fool of herself.

CHAPTER XIX: TOM TELLS THE TRUTH

Tom feels low when he gets home for lunch. But he feels even meaner and shabbier when Aunt Polly tells him she made a fool of herself boasting to Mrs. Harper all about Tom's wonderful dream, using it as proof that dreams do reveal truth, only to learn that Joe had already told his mother Tom had gone to the village that night. Tom is sorry for what he did. He answers Aunt Polly's accusation that he came to the village to laugh at her sorrow, by telling her that he came to leave a note saying that he and the other boys were well. But when he heard them discussing the funeral arrangements he got inspired, so he didn't leave the note; it should still be in the pocket of the old jacket he was wearing. Polly finds it hard to believe him this time, but she forgives him-even if he is lying - and sends him back to school with a kiss.

After Tom leaves the house, Polly is tempted to look in the jacket pocket for the note. She is afraid, however, that she won't find the note, adding to the already strong evidence that Tom has lied. Finally, telling herself that if it was a lie it was a good lie, she takes the jacket down and rifles the pockets. There is the note, just as Tom had described it. Overjoyed, she confesses through her tears: "I could forgive the boy, now, if he'd committed a million sins."

Comment: This chapter establishes Tom's essential good-heartedness, and provides a final ending to the adventure at piracy. By being placed here, it provides some relief from Tom's difficulties in his love affair, which is getting more intense and complicated. Notice that as the whole novel moves along more and more incidents are beginning to show Tom's worth and inherent nobility, even though he still does occasionally behave like a "harum-scarum" boy.

CHAPTER XX: BECKY IN A DILEMMA

Something about the way Aunt Polly kissed him makes Tom feel good on his way to school. Since he is in a good mood, he apologizes to Becky when he meets her, and promises never to be mean to her again. Becky, however, stuns Tom by telling him scornfully to keep to himself; she'll never speak to him again. Tom is so taken aback that he can't think of an insult to heave at her until the time for insults has passed. When they meet again in the schoolyard, however, they exchange barbs; Tom wishes she were a boy so he could pummel her; Becky can't wait until school is "in" so she can see Tom whipped for spoiling the spelling book. She does not know she is heading for deep trouble herself.

The teacher, Mr. Dobbins, has always wanted to be a doctor, but his family was too poor to send him to medical school. But his interest in medicine is so great, Twain tells us, that he keeps a medical textbook in his desk drawer - under lock and key - and, when the class is busy at seat work or when for some other reason there are no recitations to be heard, takes it out and reads it. He is careful to let none of the students see the book, so naturally they all are curious.

As Becky is wandering around the building she notices that Mr. Dobbins had left the key in the desk when he went home for lunch. She takes advantage of this opportunity to look at the book. Becky doesn't understand what the big word "anatomy" on the cover of the book means, so she opens the book and becomes engrossed in the picture of the naked human that graces one full page. While she is studying the picture she suddenly notices a shadow fall on the page. Tom saw her looking at the book, and walked quietly into the room to peer over her shoulder. Becky hurriedly closes the book, but in doing so she tears the page. Vexed and shamed, she pushes the book into the drawer, turns the key, and accuses Tom of making her tear the picture. She knows she will be whipped for thus destroying the teacher's picture; further, she'll be whipped in full view of the entire class. She accuses Tom of planning to squeal on her. Tom, of course, plans no such thing. He's not a squealer; he has other, more direct, ways of getting even with her for rejecting his recent apology. Besides, Tom knows there's no reason to squeal: Mr. Dobbins will ask each member of the class whether he tore the book. When he gets to Becky he'll know from the expression on her face that she's the guilty party.

Tom concludes that girls are a strange lot, to take on so about a little thing like a whipping. Still, he would like to do something to help Becky, but he can't think of anything that'll help her. She's sure to give herself away.

When school is called back "in," Tom is faced with being punished for his spoiled spelling book. He can't remember whether he spilled the ink or not, so he takes his whipping after denying the crime purely for the form of the thing. About an hour later, Mr. Dobbins goes into his desk drawer for his anatomy book. Two sets of eyes are watching him. Tom feels sorry for Becky, and tries desperately to think of some way to help her. He thinks of running to the front of the room, grabbing the book from Mr. Dobbins' hands and springing through the door with it. But before he can make his decision, Mr. Dobbins has discovered the torn page. He begins questioning the children. One by one they deny the deed. Becky, when he gets to her, almost gives herself away by not looking in his eyes when she answers. In the nick of time, Tom jumps up in his seat and shouts, "I done it." When he sees the shock on the faces of his classmates, he realizes that he has practically destroyed himself. But as he steps forward to take the punishment - the most merciless flogging ever handed out in the school - he sees gratitude and adoration in Becky's eyes, and these make the flogging worthwhile. He knows that she will even wait for him the two hours he must stay after school, and she will think the wait to be pleasant.

Tom goes to bed that night planning proper revenge against Alfred Temple, for Becky in her contrition has told Tom all. As he drifts off to sleep he remembers Becky's words: "Tom, how could you be so noble!"

Comment: Tom has made peace with both the women in his life. Somehow he has come to realize that his impulsive theatrics hurt people, especially when they are indulged in to make him the center of attention. He has learned a good use for these theatrics, though. He did not take Becky's punishment in order to be the center of attention, but rather to save Becky from painful embarrassment. In thus thinking of someone else instead of himself, Tom shows signs of growing a little. Just a little, though, because you will remember that he didn't think a whipping was such terrible punishment after all. (It is possible of course that Tom has had so many whippings that he has a thick callous under the seat of his pants.)

The incident comes to a happy conclusion. Tom is still a creature governed by his moods - he apologizes to Becky because he is feeling good; he takes her whipping on the spur of the moment. Twain suits character to action so effectively that the one always seems to flow from the other.

CHAPTER XXI: THE PUBLIC EXAMINATION

Because vacation time and the public "examination" of the students are fast approaching, the schoolmaster becomes more and more strict. The students get restless and rebel, trying in many ways to do him mischief. But he is always swift with retribution, and powerful in applying the hickory switch, for in spite of the fact that he is bald and wears a wig, he is not old and weak. "Only the biggest boys." Twain tells us, "and young ladies of eighteen and twenty, escaped lashing." The children join in conspiracy against him, enlisting the aid of the son of the village sign painter with whom the teacher boards. This boy has many grievances against Mr. Dobbins that want redressing, so he is pleased to co-operate. No one will be at home to interrupt the boy's part in the plot, which depends on Mr. Dobbins' getting "fuddled" on the dinner wine in preparation for the events of examination night, and on his dozing in his chair after supper so he'll have to leave for the schoolhouse in a hurry.

The examination day finally comes. The schoolhouse is decorated and has a festive air. The scholars are crowded into the room, those taking part on one side of the room, their parents and important village officials in another part, and the non-participating scholars in still a third section. Mr. Dobbins occupies an imposing position in the front of the room, as befits his place as head of the school. As the exercises begin, the students take their turns reciting poetry they have memorized and reading little compositions they have ground out especially for this occasion. Mark Twain discusses the qualities of some of these compositions - both prose and verse - and gives examples of them. He quotes liberally from the one that wins the first prize; it is a mushy composition, typical of the sentimental tripe written by high school girls. The audience, though, sits appreciatively through all the recitations. Mr. Dobbins is proud of his showing, and - of course - he is still a little fuddled with the dinner wine.

Revenge On Mr. Dobbins

He climbs down from his "throne" to draw a map of America on the blackboard for the geography class to work on. People in the audience begin to smile and titter because, he thinks, his hand isn't too steady. By carefully erasing and redrawing he eventually begins to get a fair representation of the country on the board. Even when he feels he's doing well, however, the tittering continues. He begins to get more nervous and self-conscious, feeling that every eye in the room is on him. But he is wrong. As he's drawing away, the trap door above his head has been opened and a cat is being lowered upon him. The cat drops slowly down, down, writhing and clutching at air with its claws, seeking a solid foothold. When it is within reach of Mr. Dobbin's head, it swipes desperately at his wig, which clings to its claws as it is pulled rapidly back up into the attic. Mr. Dobbins' head gleams in the light: the sign painter's boy had gilded it. The evening ends. The boys have had their revenge, and vacation time has begun.

Comment: Mark Twain seems to pause with this chapter to give us a breathing spell before taking up more serious matters in the story of Tom's adventures. Notice that in this very funny chapter there is no real involvement of Tom or any identification with specific students. This is the kind of incident, though, that most schoolboys would like to be involved in, for that is their nature. By making the overbearing Dobbins suffer at the hands of his young charges, Twain has developed a scene that warms the hearts of many schoolboys the world over.

The chapter is interesting because it is the vehicle of Twain's **burlesque**. In presenting selections of the compositions, Twain tells us he's quoted them from a little book, *Prose and Poetry, By a Western Lady*. There is a great similarity between these quotations and the examples of Emmeline Grangerford's poetry that Twain describes for us in *Huckleberry Finn*. While it may not seem cricket for Twain to attack what is after all sincerely meant and fairly harmless pap, we must remember that Twain uses these compositions as the main "hook" on which to hang his **burlesque** of the whole system of education and examination which taught nothing and led no one to emotional maturity.

This chapter concludes Tom's schoolday adventures. From now on, Tom is on vacation and is freer to come and go, and to become a major figure in more hair-raising adventures than those he has met with so far.

THE ADVENTURES OF TOM SAWYER

TEXTUAL ANALYSIS

CHAPTERS 22-26

CHAPTER XXII: SUMMER VACATION

Because he likes their uniforms, Tom joins a church group known as the Cadets of Temperance. He promises not to smoke, swear or drink as long as he is a member. No sooner does he pledge, than he discovers an infallible truth about human nature: to not be permitted to do a thing makes you want to do it all the more. The only thing that keeps Tom from breaking his pledge is the hope that he can parade in his red sash. July Fourth is a long way in the future, so he places his hopes on Judge Frazier, the local justice of the peace who is about to die and will very likely have a large public funeral. Tom becomes solicitous for the Judge's health, hoping it takes a turn for the worse. Word come that the Judge is getting better. Tom quits the Cadets in disgust. When the Judge dies that night, Tom loses faith in human nature. As he watches the Cadets parade in their gaudy uniforms at the fancy funeral, he notices a disconcerting thing: he no longer wants to smoke, swear or drink.

THE ADVENTURES OF TOM SAWYER

The freedom of vacation is beginning to bore him. There is nothing to do. The circus, the minstrel show and the phrenologist and mesmerizer who visit town take the edge off the boredom for a few days, but the boys find that time hangs heavy on their hands more often than not. Fourth of July is a failure: the parade is rained out, and the U. S. Senator who visits town isn't anywhere near being twenty-five feet tall as Tom had imagined such a great man would be. Moreover, Becky has gone home to Constantinople to spend the vacation with her family. There is really nothing to distract Tom from the thoughts of the murder which are always with him, making his days a chronic misery.

At this point, he is laid up for two weeks with the measles. When he is out of bed at last, he looks for his friends only to learn that a "revival" has been in town, and everyone-even Joe Harper, Ben Rogers, Jim Hollis and Huck Finn(!) - has got religion. He feels he is the only one in town whose soul is lost. That night a fierce thunderstorm keeps him awake with the fear that it has been sent to destroy him with its lightning because he is unrepentant.

The next day the measles are back, and Tom is confined to bed for three more weeks. When he finally gets up, he wanders down the street, feeling lonely and friendless in his sinfulness. Then he sees Jim Hollis acting as judge in the murder trial of a cat who killed a bird; further along he meets Huck and Joe eating a stolen watermelon. They have-like Tom-relapsed.

Comment: Mark Twain uses this chapter as transition between schooldays and mid-summer. Notice how the lack of activity because of early summer boredom and Tom's sickness keeps the story from becoming too frantic. If Tom had continued to have adventures at the rate he was having them in the early chapters of this novel, he would be a suitable candidate for our modern tranquilizer drugs. As it is, Mark Twain has made the story pause for a while and so has given us a more real-seeing picture of what a boy's life is like.

This chapter also alludes to two important themes. The first of these is Becky's absence. By this **allusion** we are reminded of Tom's involvement with Becky, and the pleasant stage that relationship has reached. The second **allusion** is to the murder. We are reminded that a great deal is going to happen in spite of this lack of action and excitement. And this is important, for Tom Sawyer is, as we have suggested several times already, something of a potboiler.

In recounting Tom's involvement with the Cadets of Temperance, Twain has prepared us for some of the adventures which will follow. Note that in spite of all the emotional growth Tom has made in some of the more recent chapters, he is still very much a boy and capable of thinking like the old Tom Sawyer we knew so well in the early chapters of this novel. Twain doesn't make Tom so suddenly into a mature young man that his change seems miraculous or contrived. By having Tom change in some ways, but not in others, Twain keeps the novel consistent and unified.

Notice also how the boys' reactions to the circus and the other visiting entertainments affect them. They are affected in just about the same way by the visit of the revival meeting. This is Mark Twain commenting on the place of religion in these people's lives: it is a brief and perhaps welcome intrusion that breaks up the monotony, but that seems to be all. In restricting his comments on the effect of the revival to its effect on the boys Twain is using a recognized **burlesque** device: writers of burlesque will often have children do what is ordinarily done by adults. In this way the writers can point up more forcefully some of the irrationality that is characteristic of human behavior. The fact that Tom and Becky as children are the major **protagonists** in this novel's **burlesque** of courtship, makes the burlesqued elements stand out much more clearly and forcefully.

Finally in this chapter, Twain **burlesques** the fear that people have that they will be punished with some sort of immediate and total divine retribution for their sins. Note how Tom becomes immensely frightened at the thunderstorm, as though Providence were interested, as Twain likes to say over and over in his books, enough in human bugs to work up all that energy just to destroy one of them when there are more economical ways of doing so. Of course, Twain speaks of superficial and superstitious concepts of religion. From the point of view of technique, by using Tom as the central figure in this **burlesque**, he can point out the innate childishness of this kind of religious experience.

CHAPTER XXIII: OLD MUFF'S FRIENDS

The village springs to life when Muff Potter's trial at last comes into court. It becomes so much the topic of conversation that Tom and Huck begin to feel more and more miserable about their secret. Their consciences bother them so much they find it necessary to swear once more to tell no one about seeing the murder. To calm their consciences, they continue to slip down to the jailhouse to give Muff tobacco and matches secretly. On this evening, the night before the trial, Muff is exceptionally grateful to the boys for they are the only people who have been kind to him. He tells them to stay away from whiskey, which was what got him into trouble, and in many other way lets them know he's thankful they haven't forgotten him. He asks them to take turns standing on each other's shoulders and to slip their hands between the window bars so he can shake their hands, "little hands, and weak-but they've helped Muff Potter a power, and they'd help him more if they could."

Tom's sleep is disturbed for the next two nights. He has frightening nightmares. The misery his conscience is causing him makes him avoid the courthouse. He won't go in, just hangs around outside, avoiding Huck Finn but listening to the conversations of the villagers to get as much information about the trial as he can. On the second day of the trial, Tom learns that Injun Joe's testimony is holding up. Muff Potter, then, is as good as hung. That night Tom is out late, and when he finally comes in through the window, he is in such a state of agitation that he cannot get to sleep.

The End Of The Trial

The next morning the whole village turns out for the final day of the trial. In the course of the proceedings, Muff's lawyer refuses to cross-examine any of the prosecutor's witnesses. The villagers wonder at the strange tactics; they have come to see a show and they are not getting one. Muff's cause looks bad when the State rests its case, indicating in its summation that Potter committed a heinous crime. Muff, who is emotionally overwrought at this point, groans aloud.

Potter's lawyer opens the case for the defense. He begins by telling the court he has decided to change his tactics. He had hinted, the first day of the trial, that his defense of Potter would be the plea that Muff acted irresponsibly under the influence of alcohol. He will change that plea. He asks the clerk to call the first witness for the defense-Tom Sawyer!

Tom is badly scared when he takes the stand. He sees Injun Joe looking right at him. Under careful and dramatic questioning, Tom begins to tell where he was the night of the murder, why he was there (laughter in the courtroom), and what he saw there. He is interrupted by the lawyer and cautioned not to mention his companion's name - there is time for that if there is need to introduce the other witness. At the moment when Tom tells the jury how he saw Injun Joe stab the doctor after Muff was knocked out, there is a sudden crash in the court-room, and Injun Joe jumps through a window, making a dramatic escape.

Comment: Notice how skillfully Mark Twain builds up the narrative to a **climax**. To all intents and purposes, Muff is going to be found guilty. Tom has made sure Huck won't talk, and he has several reasons himself for not talking: he has taken two oaths, he has tried to salve his conscience by being kind to Muff, and he is deathly afraid of Injun Joe. At the same time, what he observes and overhears in the village while the trial is going on leads him more and more to think of the injustice that is being done to Muff - who has come to believe he's killed the doctor.

Remember what was said earlier about Tom maturing when he took Becky's whipping. That ability to grow up and assume grown-up responsibility is what makes Tom able to stand up for Muff's rights. So Twain is very careful about providing believable antecedents for the major elements in the plot. He doesn't allow anything to happen without properly preparing the reader for it by setting up conditions under which it could happen. If the boys hadn't been properly afraid of Injun Joe, they might have told on him right away, and he'd probably have been captured. That would very likely have been the end of that. But, as it is, he has escaped. Now Twain can develop more adventures in which Injun Joe has a part. And, of course, the element of horror is multiplied. For, we are now certain that Tom will die if he meets Injun Joe face to face.

It is interesting that Huck doesn't seem to have kept pace with Tom in maturing emotionally. Huck is still very practical and very afraid of dying. But remember that Huck is a "child of nature" living by his wits in a world that is hostile to him. One of the first instincts of nature is that of self-preservation. And

Huck is determined to preserve himself at all costs. It is only the truly mature, social individual who can tame his instincts and rise above the call of nature as Tom had done.

CHAPTER XXIV: TOM THE VILLAGE HERO

Tom is the village hero. He is petted and praised every day. His name is in the paper, and the villagers see signs of greatness in all his actions, many of which they had disapproved of in the past. But every night, alone in his bed, he knows mortal horror. He keeps dreaming of Injun Joe. Nothing can make him leave the house after dark for fear of running into the villain.

Huck too is worried. Although he was not needed in court after Injun Joe broke out, and although the lawyer and Tom are the only persons who know he is the other witness, Huck is afraid his part in the affair will leak out. He has lost confidence in the human race, Twain tells us, when Tom's conscience drove him to break "the dismalest and most formidable of oaths."

Tom is so afraid of Injun Joe he won't rest well again until he knows Joe is dead and sees Joe's corpse. But aside from a clue discovered by a detective brought to the village from St. Louis, no hint of Joe is found. The detective goes home. Twain concludes this chapter with this sentence: "The slow days drifted on, and each left behind it a slightly lightened weight of apprehension."

Comment: Notice how the villagers change their attitudes toward Muff once someone has taken the burden of speaking out in his behalf. They can't seem to do enough for him now. And Muff, not at all ungrateful, does all he can to express his feelings to Tom. This makes Tom happy. He - like any mature individual - welcomes someone else's appreciation of what he does. Notice also that Tom doesn't brag and boast of his accomplishment. He takes the glory in his stride. At night he is worried sick.

But people can live in fear only so long. As each day passes, Tom becomes a little less fearful. This is a normal reaction - the longer we live with fear, the less anxious we are. We get used to it.

What is the tone of Twain's reference to the St. Louis detective? Why is this detective from St. Louis? Does this have any relationship to the fact that the dandy Tom beats up in the early chapters is a St. Louis boy? St. Louis is a big town; St. Petersburg is a little village. The people seem to stand in awe of Big Town sophistication as evidenced by their hiring of a detective from the Big Town in expectation of capturing Injun Joe quickly with his help. On the other hand, the villagers seem to distrust and dislike Big Town superiority - they call it "snobbishness" - as evidenced by Tom's immediate dislike for the boy he had beat up in Chapter I.

CHAPTER XXV: ABOUT KINGS AND DIAMONDS

One day Tom decides he wants to dig for buried treasure. He looks up his friends Joe Harper and Ben Rogers, but they are not around. So he finds Huck, who is willing to try anything that doesn't cost money. Before they go off, Tom must explain to Huck the theory behind treasure hunting. Huck doesn't seem to realize that the digging is the fun; he is very practical about the enterprise. Tom is willing to try to dig under every tree limb and on every island and in every haunted house he can find. He isn't worried about spending a great deal of time digging under the wrong limb. Huck stops worrying about the amount of work too, when Tom tells him that some diamonds are worth as much as twenty dollars, while most are worth at least six bits or a dollar. Kings and people like that have many diamonds, Tom says. With this remark, he must explain to Huck what kings are and why they don't hop.

They decide to dig under a dead limb tree on a hill three miles beyond the village. Once they arrive, they rest under a tree, smoke and discuss how they will spend their money. Huck will spend his money on pie and soda and circuses. He sees no reason to save any of it because his pap will come back to the village someday and get his hands on it. Tom will spend his money on a new drum, a real sword, a red necktie and a bull pup, and will use what's left over to get married on. To Huck his last is a sign that Tom is out of his mind. Huck knows how bad life was when his mother was alive - his parents fought all the time. Tom replies that the girl he'll marry won't fight. When Huck asks what's the name of the "gal," Tom replies, "It ain't a gal at all - it's a girl." Huck comments that it makes no difference, they're all the same. Tom promises to tell Huck the name of the girl someday, but not right now. They call a halt to the conversation and set about digging.

After working for an hour and not finding anything, they choose another spot and dig some more, still finding nothing. They dig most of the afternoon and still find nothing, so they decide to come back at midnight when they'll be able to see where the moon casts the shadows of the dead limb. For it is in these shadows, Tom says, that robbers bury their treasure. Returning that night, they dig some more with noises of spirits in the leaves and ghosts hiding in bushes and under trees. Still they find nothing. Tom convinces Huck to come with him to the haunted house the next day - in full daylight because spirits don't bother people then - and search for treasure.

Comment: In this chapter Twain prepares us for further adventures of Tom and Huck. Note the setting carefully. It is near Cardiff Hill, and not too far from the Widow's home. This will be important to the action in later chapters. Obviously, Tom's fear of Injun Joe is wearing thin; he thinks nothing of going out at midnight to search for buried treasure in lonely spots.

There are many similarities between this chapter and Chapter IX, where the boys go to the cemetery to cure some warts. Aside from the fact that both outings are for childish play, there are other similar elements, like the midnight hour. If we are aware of the similarities between these two chapters, we expect their outcome to be similar. But Twain varies the action somewhat by having the boys return home unmolested and peacefully.

In Chapter XXIII of *The Adventures of Huckleberry Finn*, there is a conversation between Huck and the escaped slave Jim that echoes - in overall tone - the conversation between Tom and Huck in this chapter of Tom Sawyer. In the Huck Finn **episode**, Huck takes the part Tom has in this book. Besides being humorous, the conversations tell us something about the characters who are involved in them. Notice that Tom uses words loosely - he says kings hop around - while Huck uses them literally - he wants to know why they hop. Tom's is a more literary cast of mind, Huck's is more practical. Twain develops the conversation in Huck Finn in much the same way as he develops it here. This is an illustration of how Mark Twain was able to make his stories more effective by reworking elements of them, improving them with each re-telling.

Notice how Tom, for the first and only time in the book, corrects Huck's language. The implication is that by calling Becky a "gal" Huck has somehow demeaned her. His beloved is so sacred to Tom he doesn't want to discuss her with anyone outside the pale of society as Huck is. He is happy to contemplate her by himself. A very idyllic picture this is.

CHAPTER XXVI: THE HAUNTED HOUSE

About noon the next day the boys arrive at the dead tree where they had left their tools the day before. They are ready to go to the haunted house, but Huck suddenly realizes that it is Friday, a notoriously unlucky day. Not only that but he dreamed of rats last night, and that means there's trouble in the offing. Tom agrees with Huck that it would be wise to postpone the treasure hunt. So the two of them spend the rest of the afternoon playing Robin Hood, going home when the sun begins to set. They resolve to tackle the haunted house next day, Saturday.

The following day they get to the dead tree, relax for a while, then turn a few more spadesful of earth in their last hole just to make sure they aren't missing a fortune because they don't dig deep enough. They then head for the haunted house, which they enter quietly, cautiously and curiously. They note the dirt floor with weeds growing through it, the fireplace, the unplastered walls and the rickety staircase that leads to the second floor. After exploring the downstairs, they get braver and decide to look upstairs. Throwing their tools in a corner, they climb the stairs where they find a closet which they investigate. Disappointed that the closet holds nothing, they are about to go down when Tom hears noises of men approaching the house. He tells Huck to be quiet - not even whisper - and they lie down, their eyes glued to knot-holes in the floor through which they can watch the activity below.

Injun Joe in Disguise!

Two men, a deaf and dumb Spaniard who has been seen around town a couple of times recently, and a complete stranger, enter. The boys overhear the men's conversation. The stranger wants to back out of a criminal job because it's a dangerous one. When the Spaniard argues against his fear, the boys recognize him from his voice-he is Injun Joe in disguise! They hear the men talking about how dangerous it is to use the house as a hideaway. It is too much in the open where many people can observe their coming and going. They couldn't stir all day yesterday, the stranger remarks, "with those infernal boys playing over there on the hill right in full view." The "infernal boys" thank their lucky stars that they paid attention to the omen in Huck's dream which was reinforced by the day being Friday. It certainly would have been an unlucky day to go to the haunted house. Twain remarks, "They wished in their hearts they had waited a year."

The two men settle down to eat, then discuss their projects. Injun Joe wants the stranger to go back up river to his home, while Joe spies out the dangerous job that has to be done. Then he'll call the stranger back, they'll do the job, and head for Texas together. This is satisfactory to the stranger. Joe then stretches out for a nap, leaving the stranger to stand watch. Presently the stranger falls asleep.

When Tom becomes aware that the two men are sound asleep, he tries to talk Huck into making a break for it. But Huck is too scared. He refuses. So Tom tries to go alone. He changes his mind quickly, however, when he hears how badly the floor creaks as soon as he shifts his weight a little. He decides to wait with Huck. Eventually, when the sun is just about to set, Joe awakens. He stirs his comrade, abusing him for falling asleep on guard. Then they make preparations to go. They have with them six hundred and fifty dollars in silver which they decide to bury in the house until they are ready to leave for Texas. The stranger takes twenty or thirty dollars and gives Joe a like amount to use until they come for the rest of it. The boys can't believe their luck! Here are two robbers burying a fortune right in front of their eyes. There'll be no need to hunt for the spot the treasure's buried in.

Buried Treasure

Joe digs away with his bowie knife in a corner of the house. Unexpectedly, his knife hits something solid. It's an old wooden box, half rotted away from being underground for years. Reaching his hand through the broken lid, he pulls out a handfull of gold coin-he's found a treasure! The boys upstairs are as excited as Joe and the stranger. It seems that Huck was correct in saying that robbers' treasures are buried all over everywhere.

The stranger remembers having seen an old pick and shovel lying in a corner of the house. He gets the tools-which belong to Tom and Huck - and hands them to Joe. Joe looks at the pick critically a moment, then begins digging with it. Soon he has the box out of the ground, and comments, "Pard, there's thousands of dollars here."

His comrade agrees, observing that a robber band known as "Murrel's gang used to operate in this area at one time and had probably put the gold there. He continues, "Now you won't need to do that job." Joe speaks passionately when he replies that robbery isn't the motive for the job he wants to do. Revenge is. He tells his comrade to go home, since he's afraid of getting into trouble, and wait until he hears from him. The stranger agrees again. To the great delight of the boys upstairs, the men set about burying the gold again. Just at this point Joe remembers that the pick he used had fresh dirt on it. There's no sense burying the gold her whoever left the pick can come and see freshly disturbed earth. They will take the gold and hide it in Joe's den - Number Two, under the cross.

But Joe is still not satisfied with thus outwitting whoever left the tools. He wonders whether the persons who brought them are upstairs. Tom and Huck are petrified with fear, unable to move to the relative safety of the closet as Injun Joe puts his hand to his knife and starts up the steps. There is a sudden crash and Joe lands on the ground among the ruins of the rotten stairs. He gets up cursing, and his partner tells him there's no sense trying to go up there now, since it's almost dark anyway. If anyone is courageous enough to follow them in the dark, let them. He and Joe can handle interlopers. Besides he doesn't really believe anyone is around. He tells Joe the owners of the pick and shovel probably thought he and Joe were ghosts and ran off. Joe finally agrees that they ought to use the remainder of the daylight to get their gear together. They leave, headed toward the river with the box of gold.

Tom's Fear

Tom and Huck stare after the departing thieves through cracks in the logs of the house. They then depart for the village, being careful to take the trail over the hill in back. All the way home they blame themselves for bringing the pick and shovel to the house. Without these tools, Joe would never have suspected anyone had been around, and the boys would have got the silver and the gold. They decide that they were too close to owning the treasure to give up now. They will keep a lookout for Joe and follow him to "Number Two." Then Tom thinks of something fearful. Joe spoke of revenge; suppose he meant revenge on Tom and Huck for witnessing the murder. The boys talk over this distressing idea, and decide that if anything, Joe means revenge on Tom, since Huck's part in the secret hasn't been made public yet. This is not much comfort to Tom.

Comment: Notice how carefully Twain makes all the details fit together in this chapter so that the story is not only exciting and suspenseful, but seems to follow naturally from the boys' characters and their actions. By deciding not to go to the house on Friday, the boys save themselves from being murdered. For the reader this decision means added suspense - the treasure-hunt and whatever else Twain has in store for us - is put off a few pages while the scene is set. This is accomplished by means of superstition: Friday is a bad luck day, and dreaming of rats means trouble. (Note that Huck is the one who has the dream, and that Huck believes in these two superstitions, but not necessarily in all superstitions. The reason is that Huck is a practical person who generally believes only what he has experience of. Some superstitions work. Others have no practical usefulness.)

On the other hand, note that Tom seems to be his old bookish self. When the boys go to the dead tree on Saturday, he insists on following all the "rules" of treasure hunting. So they dig a few more inches to make sure there's no treasure just beneath the point where they stopped digging. This leaves fresh dirt on the pick. The dirt makes Injun Joe suspicious, and he almost kills the boys. And, very important from the boys' point of view, he removes the treasure to a spot where they can't get at it. Be aware of this difference between Tom and Huck. It is one of the most important contrasts in the book.

Notice how Tom seems to find real adventure when he's only looking for play adventure. Notice too how Tom doesn't seem to realize that he's having a real adventure. Of course this chapter has a great deal of the melodramatic elements that characterize "potboiler" fiction. Notice how Joe gets passionate when he speaks of revenge, like a dime novel hero. And notice too, how he grasps the hilt of his knife and starts up the stairs, murder in his eye. Twain skillfully undercuts this melodrama by having Joe take the equivalent of a slap-stick pratfall when the action is at its most melodramatic. If Twain were serious about having Joe go upstairs, he wouldn't have had this clever and cruel half-breed deterred by one failure.

THE ADVENTURES OF TOM SAWYER

TEXTUAL ANALYSIS

CHAPTERS 27-30

CHAPTER XXVII: SEARCH FOR TREASURE

That night Tom dreams of his adventure. He sees the money slip through his fingers four times as he awakens during the night to realize that he missed a fortune. The next morning he finds that the whole adventure seems to be a dream. He never really thought there was such a thing in the whole world as a thousand dollars. Maybe forty or fifty dollars, but not thousands of dollars! The most he ever imagined a real treasure to be is a handful of dimes and a vague fistful of bills.

He hurries out after breakfast to meet Huck and finds him soaking his feet in the river. He waits until Huck mentions the treasure rather than broach the subject himself to make sure the events really happened and that he didn't just dream them. The boys decide to look for "Number Two." Tom investigates the two taverns in the village to see if either of them has a Room Two which might be Joe's hiding place. He finds that the less ostentatious one has a Room Two which the owner's son says is locked at all times and is probably haunted - there was a light in there last night. Tom reports this to Huck, and they conclude that this is probably the "Number Two" they're looking for. They will get all the keys they can and try them in the back door of that room, which comes out on a little alley between the tavern and the old brick store. Between now and then, however, Huck is to keep his eyes open for Injun Joe and follow him to see if he goes to that room - then the boys will be sure they're on the right track. For the money's sake, Huck agrees to this dangerous assignment.

Comment: This chapter gives us an overall view of the boy's attempt to take the treasure from Injun Joe. Notice that Tom's ingenuity takes a very practical turn here. He has the idea of trying the taverns to see which one has a Room Two. It is he who follows through on this suggestion because he doesn't want Huck to be recognized as being in unusual company, and it is he who thinks of getting all the keys they can and trying them in the door. He also seems to be the leader here, telling Huck what to do and how to do it. Huck goes along with Tom's suggestions.

By telling us that Tom thinks he dreamed the activity of the day before, Twain as much as admits that the whole affair is somewhat unbelievable. Then he reinforces the verisimilitude by having Huck speak very plainly to Tom on the chances that they have of continuing to enjoy life while they mess around in Injun Joe's affairs.

If the events of the preceding day occurred on a Saturday, then this must be Sunday. Why, then, didn't Tom's aunt scrub him up and take him off to church? In a later chapter, Twain will tell us that there is no Sunday school during the summer vacation, but he indicates that church services are held and attended as usual. In the next chapter Twain will jump from the night of this day to Tuesday. Twain apparently set the book aside for a while to let the "well of the imagination" fill up, and when he returned to it, forgot what day he stopped at. Of course, this is no great flaw in the novel, but it does serve as an illustration of the kind of blunder Twain would make because he composed by fits and starts.

CHAPTER XXVIII: AN ATTEMPT AT NUMBER TWO

That night the boys watch the tavern, but no one comes. So Tom goes home with the understanding that if Huck sees anything he will come fetch Tom. Nothing happens for the rest of that night, however, nor Tuesday and Wednesday nights, neither of which is dark enough for the boys to try to get into the room. Thursday night is better though. Tom slips out of the house with his aunt's lantern wrapped in a towel. About eleven o'clock the tavern closes. When the tavern lights are put out, the night is perfectly dark. Tom lights the lantern, blindfolds it with the towel, and creeps into the alley while Huck stands watch. Tom is gone for what seem like hours, and Huck starts down to the alley to look for him. Before he goes far, however, he meets Tom running like lightning! "Run!" said he, "run for your life!" Huck does not need further instructions. He follows Tom as they run to the deserted slaughter house, where Tom tells Huck what happened.

He tried a couple of keys, but they made a lot of noise and didn't work anyway. So he turned the knob: the door was unlocked. Stepping inside he took the towel off the lantern and, "Huck, I most stepped onto Injun Joe's hand!" Joe was lying on the floor, next to an empty bottle, sound asleep. Tom saw nothing in the room but barrels and bottles. The room, he tells Huck, is haunted with whiskey. "Maybe all Temperance Taverns have got a ha'nted room, hey, Huck?" he adds. Huck replies, "Well, I reckon maybe that's so. Who'd'a thought such a thing?" They decide not to go back because Injun Joe had drunk only one bottle, so he's probably not too sound asleep. Huck will watch the room every night from now on, though, and when he sees Joe leave, he will come for Tom and they will both spirit away the treasure.

Huck tells Tom he will be found during the day sleeping in Ben Roger's hayloft. The Rogerses let him, and so does their slave, Uncle Jake, for whom Huck carries water. Uncle Jake feeds Huck if he can spare it, Huck says, admitting that sometimes he even eats with Uncle Jake. He asks Tom not to spread that around; a fellow does some mighty peculiar things when he's hungry that "he wouldn't want to do as a steady thing."

Comment: With their discovery of "Number Two" and the obvious evidence that it is Joe's hideout, the boys get more cautious. No amount of money will help them if they get caught and killed. Notice Mark Twain's technique. He has us learn what happened in the alley room from Tom as Tom tells Huck. This, together with the storm, invests the incident with dramatic intensity because of Tom's emotional telling, which is full of concrete words and melodramatic pauses. By delaying the narration Twain also is able to heighten our interest and emotional responses.

Note the pun on the kind of spirits that haunt the back room. There certainly are spirits in the back room, but not the kind that do much haunting. This is a subtle dig at the "Temperance" movement. Did you notice the tone in Huck's reply to Tom's little remark about what seems to haunt back rooms of Temperance Taverns? It's as though Huck always knew what was in the back room, or at least isn't surprised at what is in there.

Note that so far Huck has been in the background in the action. He appears to still be looking out for the good of his own skin, letting the large share of the risks be carried by Tom. We shall see how this changes slowly in the next few chapters. The change is hinted at in Huck's comment about eating with Uncle Jake. Huck has obviously picked up his society's standards and norms here: it was unacceptable to eat at the same table with Negroes, and Huck is ashamed of doing so.

CHAPTER XXIX: THE PICNIC

Next morning, Friday, Tom hears that Judge Thatcher's family has come back to town. In his happy games with Becky and other school chums, Tom temporarily dismisses Injun Joe and the hidden treasure from his mind. At the end of the day, the children are happy to hear that Becky's mother will permit her to have the picnic on Saturday. Tom goes to bed that night, but not to sleep. He is so excited about the picnic he lies long awake, half expecting Huck to "meow," hoping he'll have the treasure to surprise Becky and the picnickers with. But no signal comes.

Saturday morning finally rolls around. About ten or eleven o'clock the children board the village ferryboat, which has been chartered to take them to Jackson's Island. The older people stay away, sending eighteen-year-old girls and twenty-three-year-old men as chaperones. Sid can't go to the picnic because he's sick, and Mary stays home to look after him. Just as the group is leaving for the boat, Mrs. Thatcher tells Becky she'd better try to stay overnight with one of her girlfriends who lives near the landing, as the group will probably be getting back from the island fairly late that night. Becky agrees, telling her mother she'll try to stay with Suzy Harper.

But Tom has other ideas. Instead of going to the Harper's, he wants Becky to join him in slipping over to the Widow Douglas' - she's known to keep plenty of ice cream on hand, and she's a very generous woman. Becky turns the suggestion over in her mind a while, then - under Tom's insistence - agrees to go. She decides not to tell anybody about the plans. Tom remembers that Huck may be calling for him this evening. But he dismisses the thought from his mind with the excuse that since there has been no call for the past several evenings, there isn't likely to be one tonight, either.

Shortly, the boat arrives at the island, and the happy children swarm ashore, running and climbing and laughing. By and by they return to base camp with good appetites, eat and loll around until it's time to go see McDougal's Cave, the great tourist attraction on the island. At first everyone is awed by the romantic and mysterious beauty of the place, but eventually they begin to play games again, and break up into small groups to go exploring. The cave is a large place, labyrinthine and tortuous. Passages run off in all directions and cross and meet. Everyone has a good time, hiding and surprising everyone else. Presently the children wander back in twos and threes to the ferryboat, which has been waiting for them at the landing for half an hour. The captain is anxious to get underway, so when the last stragglers leave the cave the boat heads for St. Petersburg without delay.

Huck Helps The Widow Douglas

Huck, meanwhile, has been watching the tavern for some time. He sees the ferryboat coming back to the village, and not knowing about the picnic, wonders why it doesn't put in at the landing where it usually does. He doesn't worry about that though, for his mind is soon taken up with other things. He has just decided to retire for the night - the tavern closed and no one came from the back room - when he hears a noise. It is the back door of Number Two being closed cautiously. In a moment, two men pass him, one carrying something that looks like a box! Should he run and call Tom? There isn't time for that. If the box contains the treasure, by the time Huck gets Tom the men will be away and gone and the boys will never see the gold again. Huck follows.

The men go three blocks along the river, then turn left up a cross street and head straight until they come to the path that leads up Cardiff Hill. They keep going up this, past the Welshman's house, and continue climbing. Huck is elated. He thinks the men are going to bury the box in the old quarry, where it'll be easy for him and Tom to find. But the men don't stop there. They keep going, further and further in the dark night, which makes Huck have to close up the distance between them. When they finally stop, Huck realizes where they are: not five steps from the Widow's stile. Again Huck is elated. If they are going to bury the treasure here, he and Tom will find it easily. But the men don't bury the treasure. Instead, they start to talk about the job they are about to do. Huck is badly shaken when he realizes from the sound of their voices that he is no more than a few feet from them and is hidden only by the pitch blackness of the night and the bushes. Joe curses when he sees lights on in the house. This means the Widow has company, and they will not be able to do the job until the company leaves. The stranger suggests they forget this job, and head for Texas. But Joe gets angry and insists that he will do this job and get his revenge. He's going to tie the Widow to her bed and slit her nostrils and notch her ears, like a sow. Her husband, who was once Justice of Peace, jailed Joe and had him horsewhipped in public. And Joe will have his revenge.

Overhearing this conversation, Huck is horrified. He knows he must get help for the Widow; she has been kind to him in the past. Cautiously, with skill born of long experience, Huck tiptoes backward away from the villains. When he's far enough from them, he turns tail and runs down the hill until he reaches the Welshman's. He awakens the man and his two sons and pleads to be let in. When he learns who's knocking so fearfully in the middle of the night, the Welshman says: "Huckleberry Finn, indeed! It ain't a name to open many doors, I judge!" But because of Huck's obvious distress, he opens the door to learn Huck's troubles. It takes three minutes, after Huck has gasped out his story, for the men to arm themselves and be on their way to the Widow's stile. Huck follows them a short distance, then hides behind a rock while they go on. Suddenly there is a great deal of shooting, and someone cries out. Huck jumps to his feet and runs back down the hill, away from the action as fast as he can.

Comment: Notice how Mark Twain uses details in this chapter to build up our interest in the narrative, and to prepare for the final resolution of the three stories. First, he has the picnic occur on the same day that Injun Joe and the stranger decide to go to the Widow's house. We learn this after we have learned that Tom and Becky are planning to visit the Widow, instead of going to Mrs. Harper's overnight as Becky's mother thinks she is going to do. The result is that we think Tom and Becky are in danger from Injun Joe-after all, the Widow does appear to have company. So, we never notice that no mention is made of Tom and Becky when the ferryboat loads up and goes home. We assume, as do all the rest of the passengers and the chaperones, that Tom and Becky are on board the boat.

We assume one series of actions will occur, but Mark Twain has prepared us for another by including several apparently useless details. He tells us that Sid and Mary don't go on the picnic, and he describes the entertainments in the cave in some detail. The point of these details is that with Sid and Mary absent from the party, and with all the confusion of the games in the labyrinths of the cave, it is possible that no one is paying particular attention to Tom's whereabouts.

The description of the happy group setting out on its excursion is an idyllic one which recalls the bright carefree days of youth. It is this kind of description that makes the book an effective "hymn to boyhood."

Notice Huck's apparent change in character here. Ordinarily, when he and Tom are in a tight spot, he wishes that he was nowhere near where he happens to be, so he won't have the knowledge that he has. He seems to be essentially a coward, afraid to divulge information he has picked up because he's afraid of the harm that might come to him. He successfully controlled his conscience, you will remember, in the Muff Potter **episode** because he was afraid of what Joe would do to him. But here, under the influence of his desire to get the money, he is brave enough to follow Joe and the stranger. When he overhears their discussion, he knows he must tell on them in order to save the Widow's life. So, in spite of the risk to his own life, he runs back to the Welshman's and gasps out his horrible tale. All he asks is that no one tell who told. Moreover, as Tom will tell Sid in a later chapter, Huck is essentially brave as well as goodhearted: not every boy would have gone for help. Some boys would have been so scared and so hateful they would have left the Widow in the villain's hands.

The fact that Huck behaves in a mature way is developed by his running away when the shooting starts. He is deathly afraid of Injun Joe. Yet, in spite of this fear for his own skin, he had tried to help the Widow. When he can do no more for her, and when her safety is put in the hands of someone who can protect her, he immediately removes himself from danger.

CHAPTER XXX: THE WELSHMAN REPORTS

At the earliest moment of dawn on Sunday, Huck crawls carefully up the hill to the Welshman's. He knocks gently at the door, and identifies himself when asked. The Welshman, learning that it's Huck Finn, replies: "It's a name that can open this door night or day, lad! - and welcome!" (Huck cannot remember anybody saying "welcome" to him before.) The Welshman tells Huck to relax while breakfast is being made. He and his boys had hoped Huck would stay at their house last night after the incident. Huck confesses that he got scared and ran three miles before he stopped. He's come back now only to find out what happened. The Welshman tells Huck that the desperadoes got away in the dark when he sneezed at the wrong time and alarmed them by shooting too soon. He and his boys chased them for a time, then, when they lost the track in the dark night, rousted out the constables who have organized a posse to guard the riverbank. As soon as its properly light out, the sheriff and his men will search the woods. He asks Huck for a description of the men, which Huck supplies. He does not tell the Welshman what he knows of the identity of the deaf and dumb Spaniard, for he is still afraid the Welshman will not keep secret the source of information. Indeed, he makes the man's sons promise - as they leave to join the posse - not to tell anyone where they got the information they have. He says that he knows too much about one of the desperadoes and would not want the man to find out.

Huck's Story

Presently, the Welshman asks Huck how he came to follow the villains. Huck makes up a story about not being able to sleep the night before he had got to thinking how useless he was and how he ought to try to make something of himself-so he went wandering around the town. Well, when he "got to that old shackly brick store by the Temperance Tavern, I backed up again the wall to have another think." Just then the two men passed him. They stopped to light up their cigars, and in the glow of the tips, Huck recognized the deaf and dumb Spaniard and the ragged stranger. He followed them because they had a package he thought might have been stolen goods. When they came to the Widow's, the ragged one argued to let the widow alone, while the deaf and dumb Spaniard swore he'd spoil her looks.

The Welshman interrupts Huck's story: "What! the deaf and dumb man said all that!" Huck realizes he's on the verge of giving away the secret of who the Spaniard really is. Yet, he's so afraid of Injun Joe, he tries to lie. But he's unsuccessful. He has to tell the Welshman the truth, but he does so only after extracting the Welshman's promise not to tell where he learned it. The Welshman realizes that no white man would speak of doing the terrible things to the Widow that the Spaniard has spoken of, so Huck must be telling the truth: the terrible method of taking revenge is characteristic of half-breeds.

During breakfast Huck almost betrays his real purpose for following the two men when he gets excited as the Welshman mentions that his boys captured a bundle from the thieves. It turns out, however, that the bundle contained burglary tools. But the Welshman, sensing there's more to the story than Huck has told, badgers him for information. When asked what he thought the bundle contained, Huck answers feebly, "Sunday-school books, maybe." The Welshman, who has a lively sense of humor, roars over this for a few minutes, then remarks that Huck doesn't look good, sort of tired and pale. Perhaps this is why Huck isn't thinking straight. Huck, however, is glad the treasure hasn't been found. Now he and Tom will have a chance to search "Number Two" carefully without trouble or fear.

At that moment there is a knock at the door. Huck hides while the Welshman admits the Widow and a group of ladies and gentlemen. The news of the night's excitement has spread, and these people have come to thank the Welshman who passes off the thanks, telling the visitors that the gratitude is due to someone else who doesn't want to be known. The Widow indicates that she had fallen asleep while reading in bed that night, and had slept all through the noise and excitement.

The Next Morning

Everyone is early for church that morning, even though there is no Sunday school during vacation time, discussing the previous night's excitement. After services, Mrs. Thatcher asks Mrs. Harper when Becky will be getting up.

She learns that Becky didn't go there the night before. When Polly comes to ask Mrs. Harper whether Tom stayed with Joe that night, all three women become anxious. Tom and Becky are missing. A crowd gathers around the women. In a short time someone suggests that Tom and Becky are still in the cave! In a moment the news travels and within half an hour over two hundred men are making their way to the island to search for the children in the cave. The search goes on all day and all night Sunday, Monday and Tuesday. Only hints of Tom and Becky's presence in the cave are found: one of Becky's hair ribbons, and "Becky And Tom" traced on the wall with candlesmoke. Once again the village is thrown into despair; the villagers lose interest in everything. Even the scandalous discovery of liquor in the Temperance Tavern does not cause a stir of excitement.

Hunk, in the meantime, is lying feverish and racked with delirium in the Welshman's house and is being nursed by the Widow. He awakens occasionally and tries to find out whether the treasure has been found. He asks the Widow about the Tavern, and is glad to learn that only the whiskey has been discovered. He's sorry to learn that the treasure seems gone forever, and also finds it curious that the Widow should cry. He does not connect her crying with the fact that he has mentioned Tom Sawyer. This is Tuesday afternoon, the Widow is thinking, and there aren't many people left with the hope or the means to go on searching for the children.

Comment: A great deal happens in this chapter. Notice how Twain has kept up the promise of the suspense he's been building. Tom and Becky didn't go to the Widow's after all. So our expectation that they would meet Injun Joe and the stranger is dashed. We seem to have been "sold," as Huck would put it, only to be rewarded with a greater adventure. What is going to happen to Tom and Becky who are lost in the cave?

Mark Twain seems to have run into a problem at the end of this chapter. In general, the action in this book seems to follow neatly from believable antecedents which prepare us for whatever happens. But, now that Tom is lost, and Injun Joe is scared off, what will Huck do? Well, Twain has to mark time until the rest of the story catches up to Huck. So he has Huck get very sick. But note that it is necessary for Huck to get sick suddenly - you can't go chasing criminals for a week if you're half dead; you see there isn't time here for Huck to get sick slowly, or to feel the illness coming on. As a result the illness appears to be a mechanically contrived incident to help pass time away. (Remember that Twain has done this before in this novel, when he had Tom come down with the measles in order to pass time at the beginning of the vacation until Muff Potter's trial.)

But Twain hides this mechanical contrivance by investing it with other purposes than the most important one of passing time. Through it he builds up suspense by having Huck deliriously ask about the treasure, and wanting to know if Tom has been the one who discovered Number Two.

THE ADVENTURES OF TOM SAWYER

TEXTUAL ANALYSIS

CHAPTERS 31-35

CHAPTER XXXI: TOM AND BECKY IN THE CAVE

This chapter returns to Tom and Becky at the picnic. When the two begin to tire of the hide and seek games the children are playing, they wander away on an exploring trip of their own. At first Tom makes smoke marks to direct them on their return journey. But they encounter a roomful of bats, and run into several passages without marking their path. They continue wandering, enthralled by the great natural beauty of the cave, until Becky remarks that they are now so far away from the rest of the children she can no longer hear their shouts and laughter. They do not know how long they've been gone so they decide to start back. But they can't find the way. When Becky breaks down and cries, Tom blames himself for not being careful and making marks, but Becky plucks up her spirits and says she will follow him if only he doesn't talk that way again. They wander this way and that, looking for a way out. Presently, Tom takes Becky's candle and blows it out. She recognizes this as a sign that Tom feels they may be lost in the cave for a long time, for she knows he has a pocket full of candles, yet he is saving every little piece he can.

Becky becomes tired and sleeps a while, for which Tom is grateful because her face becomes smooth and relaxed in sleep and she smiles as though her dreams are pleasant ones. When she awakens she says, without thinking, that the dream was so pleasant she wishes she could sleep forever. But she takes back the words when she sees the guilty look on Tom's face. They try again to find a way out, but they find they must rest, and look for water. Presently, Tom takes a piece of cake out of his pocket - their "wedding cake" - and they share it. After they've eaten, Becky wants to move on, but Tom tells her they must stay where they are. The little piece of candle burning itself out now is their last piece of candle. They must stay near their water. They realize that searchers would probably be looking for them by this time, but then they realize that they might not be missed till late Sunday morning, for no one knows what their plans for the night were to be. Together they watch in frightful fascination as the candle burns itself out and they are left in utter darkness.

They sleep for they don't know how long, and awakening, are miserable again. Tom can't bear to have Becky so hopelessly silent. To no avail, he tries to cheer her up. Finally, they eat the last morsel of cake, but it only teases and does not satisfy their appetites.

Sometime later, Tom hears shouting in the distance. The searchers are coming! They try to get to the noise, but come to a place where the trail seems to end on the edge of a deep pit. They cannot get across - especially since they have no candles to see by - so they must return to their water supply and wait until the searchers reach them. Tom conjectures it must be Tuesday by now.

An Unexpected Discovery

To have something to do, he decides to explore some side passages that are near at hand. He ties one end of a bit of kite string he has to a rock outcropping, and unwinding the string as he goes, he gropes along, leading Becky. About twenty steps from their starting point, the path drops off sharply. Getting down on his hands and knees, he feels for the bottom but finds none, neither in front of him nor around the corner as far as his hands can reach. As he's trying to stretch himself further to his right, he looks up to see a hand holding a candle not twenty yards away. Thinking they've been found, he lets out a joyful shout, only to see that the body the hand belongs to is Injun Joe's. Joe darts away quickly, and Tom is glad Joe didn't take the opportunity to kill him for testifying in defense of Muff Potter. He reasons that the echoes in the cavern must have disguised his voice. Afraid of running into Joe again, Tom decides to stay by the spring for good. He tells Becky, who, being around the corner, didn't see Joe, that he shouted "for luck."

After another long wait and another long sleep, Tom decides he must explore again, whether Injun Joe is around the corner or not. Becky will stay behind - she's extremely tired - and Tom will come back every once in a while to see her. He kisses her, and bravely pretends confidence in finding either the searchers or a way out of the cave. Then he takes the string and crawls away, hungry and frightened by the thought of impending death.

Comment: Most of Tom's exploring has been play-acting. This is the first time it's for real. Notice how he reacts maturely and wisely in this stressful situation.

Notice how Twain has drawn the several adventures of Tom Sawyer together in this chapter. He has Tom and his beloved lost in a cave inhabited only by Tom's mortal enemy Injun Joe, who figures in the murder story and the treasure hunt **episodes** of this novel.

Pay particular attention to the way Twain builds suspense. By ending this chapter here, he leaves us asking what is going to happen now that the children are alone with Injun Joe. Actually, nothing happens, but we are to believe something might happen.

CHAPTER XXXII: TOM TELLS THE STORY OF THEIR ESCAPE

As Tuesday comes and goes in the village, the people become more and more forlorn. The Judge hasn't been back from the cave since early Sunday, and he is there now with the handful of men who haven't given up hope. Mrs. Thatcher grows delirious with grief, and Aunt Polly settles into melancholy. That night the villagers go to bed sad.

But in the middle of the night the bells ring out joyfully, and shouts ring out from the street - "They're found! They're found!" Nobody goes to bed again that night. Tom lies on the sofa telling the curious crowds the adventure, and how, despairing, he followed two passages as far as the string would reach. Then when he went as far as he could on the third and was about to turn back, he saw daylight. Groping his way toward it, he found the light came through a small hole. He pushed his shoulders through the hole and saw below him the broad Mississippi. He tells how he went back to Becky and had to argue to convince her that he really had found a way out of their predicament. Then the two of them left the caves and were taken off the island by men passing in a skiff who rowed them to a house on shore, fed them, and made them rest a couple of hours before bringing them home.

It was dawn before Judge Thatcher and his handful of men were able to be found and brought back to the village by the messengers who carried them the good news. But it was several days before Tom and Becky recuperated enough to be able to go out again. They were kept in bed Wednesday and Thursday. Becky was not out of the room until Sunday, though Tom was able to go down to see Huck on Friday when he learned of Huck's illness. He wasn't allowed in Huck's room till Monday, when he was warned not to get Huck excited. The Widow stood by to make sure of that.

He learned from others of the events at Cardiff Hill, and that the body of the strange man had been found in the river. About two weeks after he was rescued, Tom stops by the Thatcher's to see Becky on his way to visit Huck. The Judge and several of his friends are there, and ask Tom whether he'd like to go to the cave again. When Tom replies that he would, the Judge tells him he had thought as much. That is why he had the doors of the cave repaired and sheathed with boiler iron and triple locked. Tom faints. When he's revived, he cries, "Oh, Judge, Injun Joe's in the cave."

Comment. Notice how Twain effectively tells the story of the adventure in the cave, and the way that Tom and Becky are saved. In the preceding chapter Twain went backward in his narrative. That is, in Chapter XXX he told us what the villagers were doing between Sunday and Tuesday. In Chapter XXXI he told us how Tom and Becky were faring between Sunday and Tuesday. This is a rare instance of Mark Twain's backtracking from the omniscient author point of view. Ordinarily, when it's necessary for him to go back and fill the reader in, he does so by having the characters tell each other what went on. In this way he adds dramatic interest to the story, for the observations are colored by the character's attitudes and motives. But in Chapters XXX and XXXI he does not do this;

he reserves this technique for only one part of the backtracking, that is for the part which Tom tells of after the rescue. Now, notice that we don't get a great deal of detail in this section. We get just enough information to round out the story. The reason is that the **climax** has come already - when the village bells rang out - and anything that follows it would be just overdrawing the story. Twain lets us down rapidly after the **climax**; we are now free, no longer bound by the story. Moreover, by thus summarizing briefly Tom's report on how he and Becky escaped, Twain seems to suggest that Tom is treating this return from the dead a little differently from the way he treated his earlier return with Huck and Joe from Jackson's Island.

At any rate, in resolving the action in this unusual sequence, Twain gives us an opportunity to enter into the joyful spirit of the village, which in this instance is much more dramatic than a simple narrative of Tom and Becky's relief would be.

What Twain is doing in these last few chapters is gathering up all the loose ends of the adventures. Notice how carefully he will resolve them all in Chapter XXXIV.

CHAPTER XXXIII: THE FATE OF INJUN JOE

Quickly, The Judge organizes a posse of the villagers and leads them to the cave. Tom goes with them to act as a guide. They don't need him, however, for when they get to the island and swing the great doors of the cave open, they see Injun Joe, lying there dead. He had tried to get out by cutting through the heavy timbers under the door, but broke his knife. The posse notices how, while he was slowly dying of starvation, Joe had eaten all the scraps of candle wax that tourists had left there, and a couple of bats he had managed to catch. His was a particularly slow and horrible death. They bury him near the mouth of the cave, and his grave becomes an attraction for tourists seeking the sensational.

Mark Twain comments upon the fact that after Joe's burial - which was particularly well attended (most people got as much fun out of it as they would have got out of a hanging), the petition to pardon Joe which a committee of sappy women was circulating was stopped. Twain lashes out at the "weaklings ready to scribble their names to a pardon petition, and drip a tear on it from their permanently impaired and leaky waterworks" - weaklings who would sign for Satan himself.

The morning after the funeral, Tom and Huck have a long talk. They have heard from other people quite a bit about each other's adventures, but have not had an opportunity to discuss the treasure. Huck fills Tom in on the details of his adventure - he has kept secret the part dealing with the treasure - and adds the he reckons the treasure is lost to them.

The Treasure Found

Tom excites Huck by telling him the money was never in "Number Two"; it's been in the cave all this time. He and Huck will go for it this afternoon, because Tom's the only one who knows how to get into the cave by the short cut he escaped through.

Shortly after noon, the boys "borrow" a skiff and float down to the island. Huck is still too weak to walk much more than a mile, so all the physical exertion is left pretty much up to Tom. He leads Huck into the small opening - which he says will be the hideout for his Robber Gang when he gets it organized - and shows Huck the drop in the path where he saw Injun Joe's hand.

He sees himself, now that he has a candle, that the drop is really no more than a steep hill. Then he shows Huck a smoke mark he found on the cavern wall: the cross Injun Joe was talking about! The boys clamber over to it and search carefully. Aside from some rubbish, they find nothing. Not to be deterred this close to success, Tom begins digging in what appears to be an unlikely spot, the foot of the huge rock under the cross. But he has noticed that only one side of the rock is not bespattered with candle grease and in only that area is the ground not marred with boot marks. A few inches down he strikes wood. There are planks laid over the top of a tunnel that leads under the rock, into a small passage. Tom and Huck follow the winding passage to a snug little cave where they find an empty powderkeg, a couple of guns in leather cases, a couple pairs of old leather moccasins, a leather belt, and some more rubbish, together with the treasure. After excitedly running their hands through the money for a few minutes, they put the money in the bags Tom has brought, and take it up to the large rock. Tom decides not to brings the guns up, but rather to leave them in the cave for use later when they get involved in robberies of their own. (They will use the cave a lot, Tom says, even for orgies. When Huck asks what orgies are, Tom replies that he doesn't know, but robbers have to have them.) They haul the money to the skiff, where they have a snack before going back to the village, arriving just after dark.

Tom "borrows" a wagon, puts the money in, covering it with rags. They will take the money to the loft of the Widow's woodshed, and will count it up, divide it, and bury it the next morning.

On the way to the Widow's, however, they pause to rest near the Welshman's house. The Welshman comes out just as they are about to move on, and tells them to follow him: they are wanted at the Widow's house. To speed the trip, he offers to pull the wagon. It is heavier than he realized it would be, so he asks whether it contains bricks or old metal. Tom answers truthfully, "Old metal."

When they get to the Widow's, they are surprised to learn that a party is in progress. Everyone of any importance in town is there. The Widow receives the boys gladly, and takes them upstairs where she shows them new suits of clothes which they are to change into.

Comment: With the **climax** of the treasure hunt story in this chapter, the adventures are just about over. All the odds and ends are being pulled together. Notice how Tom continues to act secretively in taking Huck to get the treasure. In many ways he is still the romantic child he was in the early chapters of the novel. But he has at least learned something about caves: this time he prepares himself properly before going in there.

Note that Tom is going to use the cave for his Robber Gang. In this Tom has not grown up, in spite of all the real adventures he has had. Even after he finds the treasure - which is, after all, a wealth undreamed of - he thinks in terms of bookish games of robbers. This is made clear in a short conversation in which Tom tells Huck that they will use the cave as a place to hold prisoners for ransoming, and as a place to hold orgies in. Although Tom explains correctly what ransoming is, he admits to Huck that he does not know what orgies are. Tom obviously does not want real adventures; he seems to want only the aura of adventures.

(In a similar passage in Huck Finn, Twain points out the same characteristic of Tom Sawyer. In the passage, Tom says that they will have to hold prisoners for ransom. When asked what ransoming is, he explains that he isn't too sure, but he rather thinks it has something to do with using hatchets to bash in prisoners' brains. The way the scene is developed in Huck Finn seems much more satisfactory, indicating that Twain did benefit by rehearsing his material over and over again in more than one story.)

Note Twain's satirical comments in this chapter on the insignificance of Man in relation to Nature, and on the "weakling" who would pardon the devil himself. This is an indication, of course, that the book was meant for more than purely children's ears.

CHAPTER XXXIV: SPRINGING A SECRET

Left alone to get cleaned up and into the new clothes, the boys react in their characteristic ways: Tom anticipates the excitement of the party, while Huck wants to climb out the window and "slope." Sid, who comes into the room while Tom is promising to help Huck get through the uncomfortable evening, tells Tom that the party is in honor of the Welshman, for his part in saving the Widow's life. The Welshman plans to surprise the whole assemblage by telling them of Huck's part in the rescue. But, Sid continues, the surprise won't be much of a surprise; he overheard the Welshman telling Aunt Polly his plans and spread the word to all the guests himself. Tom cuffs Sid for being so mean as to spoil the Welshman's surprise, and kicks him out of the room, daring him to squeal to Polly.

Sometime later, at the dinner table, the Welshman makes his speech, which is received with polite but feigned surprise. (Sid has done his sneaky work well.) Everyone gathers around Huck to compliment him and show their gratitude to him. The Widow promises to take Huck in and educate him and set him up in business when the time comes. Tom interrupts: "Huck don't need it. Huck's rich."

Of course, the people think Tom is pulling another one of his tricks. So he goes out to the wagon and returns a moment later struggling under the weight of the bags of money. He pours the coin over the table, and tells the whole story of the successful treasure hunt. The money is counted. It comes to a little over twelve thousand dollars. Twain comments: "It was more than anyone present had ever seen at one time before, though several persons were there who were worth considerably more than that in property."

Comment: Notice the contrast between Tom and Sid in the early part of this chapter. Tom dislikes Sid for the sneaky way he went about stealing the Welshman's secret. Notice too how Huck is accepted in society even before it is known that he is wealthy. Courage and good heartedness are rewarded.

CHAPTER XXXV: A NEW ORDER OF THINGS

It goes without saying that during the next couple of weeks the villagers take apart every abandoned house in the area. But no other treasures are found. Twain comments that these were not romantic children who set off on these treasure hunts, but solid, down-to-earth grown men.

Tom and Huck became the objects of admiration and attention. Their backgrounds were searched by avid admirers who suddenly discovered that the boys always had the seeds of greatness in them.

The Widow puts Huck's money out at six percent, and Aunt Polly has Judge Thatcher do the same with Tom's. Each boy now gets a dollar a day spending money, and fifty cents every other Sunday. This is more than they can possibly spend, and it is more than the minister gets. The Judge thinks Tom will be a great man someday, as famous - he tells Becky - as George Washington. (And Becky runs straight to Tom with these words.) The Judge begins planning to send Tom first to the National Military Academy and afterward to law school.

Huck Finn is taken under the Widow's protection, like it or not. He now must learn to behave himself, eat with a fork and spoon, not scratch in public, and the like. Three weeks later he turns up missing. A village-wide hunt is unsuccessful in locating him, but Tom, who understands Huck, searches him out among the hogsheads down by the abandoned tannery. Huck is miserable in civilization. He's decided to give it all up for his old freedom.

Tom tells Huck he won't be eligible for membership in the Robber Gang unless he can put up a show of respectability. Huck, who really wants to get into the Gang, agrees to go back, especially since the initiation ceremony will be as gaudy as the one Tom describes. Huck concludes: "... that's something like! Why, it's a million times bullier than pirating. I'll stick to the widder till I rot, Tom; and if I git to be a reg'lar ripper of a robber, and everybody talking 'bout it, I reckon she'll be proud she snaked me in out of the wet."

The book ends with a "Conclusion" in which Twain indicates that the story must end now because it's the story of a boy. He tells us that most of the people on whom the characters are based are still alive, and it may be interesting to someday take up the story of their lives to see what sort of men and women they turned out to be.

Comment: Note how Tom takes it upon himself to champion the cause of the civilization he has been seeking freedom from. His attitude has changed a great deal. From first trying to break away from society by thinking of being an Indian chief or pirate or robber, Tom now convinces Huck to join the very society that restricts individual freedom kin favor of the general freedom of the whole society. This is a mature and principled attitude. Tom even holds out the promise of membership in the Robber Gang as inducement for Huck to come back to civilization. The Robber Gang, looked at from this point view, is really no more than a glorified social club, something like the Masonic Orders or the Elks and Rotary.

What he's trying to point out to Huck is that being civilized is not always "worry and worry, and sweat and sweat, and a-wishing you was dead all the time."

THE ADVENTURES OF TOM SAWYER

CRITICAL BATTLE OVER MARK TWAIN'S PSYCHE

In the very early days, when Twain was still very much alive and writing, critics scorned his books, and libraries banned them for their vulgarity and "lack of consequence." Other of his contemporary critics praised him as the soul of American humor. In popular esteem, however, Mark Twain rode high, wide and handsome. He earned a fortune satisfying the tastes of the "great American populace" of the nineteenth and early twentieth centuries, while some segments of the intellectual leadership of the country looked on him with feelings of distaste that amounted almost to revulsion. In the main, Twain was revered "as America's funny man," and even after his death his work continued to command the respect of the majority of Americans.

EARLY OPINION

Some years after Twain's death in 1910, however, literary theorizing set in. Critics seemed to be less interested in what he wrote than in why he didn't write something else. Whether these theories resulted from a surfeit of Freud or from the wave of "anti-patriotism" that grew up in the twentieth century's disenchanted teens, or whether the theories arose from a mixture of these two and more, will probably never be known. At any rate, the major problem confronting students of Mark Twain's writings has come to be known as "Mark Twain's Wound."

BROOKS AND DE VOTO

In 1920 the critic Van Wyck Brooks published a volume entitled *The Ordeal of Mark Twain*. The work is based on Brooks' belief that the late-nineteenth and early-twentieth century cultural environment in America was not capable of sustaining artistic minds and helping them to grow and produce. Brooks' theory, simplified, is that the American cultural scene was too crassly materialistic to produce writers of great significance. He believed that important American literary men had to separate themselves from their native surroundings in order to allow their talents full room for development. Men like Henry James left America for other soils and climates more congenial to intellectual and artistic pursuits. Men like Ralph Waldo Emerson continued to live here, but separated themselves in spirit from strictly American ideals. They refused to restrict themselves to the intellectual attitudes narrowly characteristic of their native land.

In addition to these cultural drawbacks, Twain suffered from psychological experiences which left their mark on his sensitive personality. Further, Brooks felt that Mark Twain was a gifted writer, a man with a great talent, but a man who, unfortunately, had never allowed himself to develop his talent fully.

Searching Twain's biography, Brooks and his followers concluded that Mark Twain had chosen to gain popularity among the masses as "America's funny man," rather than to develop his skill as a serious writer. Twain's lifelong pursuit after riches and popularity was based on the not-necessarily-true American belief that wealth plus popularity equal success. That Twain chased riches is evident from the fact that he made much money which he invested in an unusual and striking house, and in business ventures (that often had little chance of success: an indication that Twain was no businessman, what he may have thought to the contrary notwithstanding). He rode to riches more than once in his lifetime. Each time he did so by becoming the "darling" of the popular audience. But by trying to appeal to the mass audience, Twain degraded himself so that he was unable to write the "serious literature" he had it in him to write. The fault lies with the society which holds up the demon "wealth" as its badge of success.

Brooks and his followers s w other forces as contributing to the repression of Mark Twain's critical artistic skill. Among these were his wife's censorship and delicate literary prudery, and his friend's (William Dean Howells) insistence that he had a great comic talent. Not least of the stunting forces were Mark Twain's boyhood and young manhood days in Southern and Western backwaters among narrow, crude, and provincial people-including his own family, which unsuccessfully chased the rabbit of success like a pack of crippled hounds.

Writers who sided with Brooks in his comments were men like Waldo Frank, Malcolm Cowley, and Upton Sinclair.

DEFENSE OF TWAIN

Shortly after the appearance of Brooks' work, however, voices began to be heard in defense of Twain's artistry. These defenders held that far from being corrupted by his surroundings, Twain was helped by them. Mark Twain did not think America was crass and vulgar. Far from it; he considered American democracy and the spirit of free enterprise to be better systems than any the world had ever produced. It is obvious that he would not turn his barbed wit against the institutions he respected most. He did turn it against social institutions that he understood to be not honorable and not good. This is as much as we can expect from any man: that he be true to his ideals, whether they correspond to those of his society and age, or not.

Men like Carl Van Doren, Henry Seidel Canby, William Lyon Phelps, and Stephen Leacock took issue with Brooks' work. Their criticism ranged from Van Doren's remarks that Brooks had tried to psychoanalyze Twain and had failed, to Leacock's basic attitude that the West made Twain an artist, with the implication that without the West Twain would have been no artist.

Not until 1932, however, did anyone undertake a full scale frontal attack on Brooks' position. In that year, Bernard De Voto, in a book called *Mark Twain's America*, took the position that Twain was a writer of a specific kind of humor: the kind that was found in the works of Petroleum V. Nasby and Artemus Ward, the boisterous local humor of the American West. The loudness and brashness of Twain's work is due to the attitude of the Western frontiersman who not only loved the world and all that he saw in it, but also saw through to the realities of things with eyes uncluttered by the confusing forms that closed up the eyes of more pretentious Eastern writers.

The critical battle lines were drawn between critics who saw Twain as a successful-if superficial-humorist, and those who saw him as a tragic figure ironically hamstrung by the society whose adulation he craved and won.

RESOLUTION OF CRITICAL WAR

By 1975 the issue seemed to be settled in De Voto's favor. If Mark Twain was not a classical example of well-adjusted humanity, neither was he a classic psychiatric basket case.

A valuable survey of the war between Brooks and De Voto is *Lewis Leary's Casebook on Mark Twain's Wound*, New York, 1962. Leary provides an introduction and survey of the problems, as well as generous selections from the writings of the critics who became involved.

Hudson Long also summarizes the dispute in his *Mark Twain Handbook*, New York, 1957, and in "Twain's Ordeal in Retrospect," *Southwestern Review* (1963), pp. 338–348.

Richard H. Powers agrees with Brooks in his "To Mark Twain's Missionary Defenders," *Forum* (1965), pp. 10–17. So does J. R. Vitelli in his "Introduction" to the 1970 reprint of Brooks' *The Ordeal of Mark Twain* (New York: E. P. Dutton).

CRITICAL REPUTATION OF "HUCKLEBERRY FINN"

The most important critical studies of Mark Twain's literary craftsmanship in the last thirty years have focused on *Huckleberry Finn*. The novel has come a long way from the days it was banned from the Concord (Mass.) Public Library for being "coarse," "inelegant," and "the veriest trash." Indeed, it draws more critical attention than any other work of Twain's.

HISTORY OF COMPOSITION

Walter Blair, for example, studied the chronological history of its composition, from the perspective of a critic interested in what was written and how it was done. His study (*Mark Twain and Huck Finn*, Berkeley: University of California Press, 1960) provides answers to many of the charges of literary bumbling and grossness brought against Twain in times past.

THE RIVER

No reader of *Huckleberry Finn* can be unaware of the tremendous flow of the Mississippi River. Some critics, notably T. S. Eliot and Lionel Trilling, have gone so far as to see in the River a kind of symbolic deity, a power sufficient to itself. The River "is not ethical or good," Trilling says, but it helps goodness grow in those people who make it an important element in their lives. It is from this general idea that Trilling develops the thesis that Huck is a servant of the River god.

Eliot maintains that the River dominates the structural form of the novel. The River is used metaphorically, structurally and thematically. Huck sees the big River gliding by and is suffused with a sense of awe and majestic calm. All the adventures begin and end on the River. Jim's freedom - the central point of the novel-involves a journey down the River. But at the same time the River does not determine Jim's freedom, Miss Watson does. And she represents the unthinking pietism and false values that Huck flees from not once, but twice: once when he leaves the Widow's house, and once again when he "lights out" for the Indian territory ahead of the rest because the Phelpses want to adopt him.

Both Eliot and Trilling use their conclusions to justify the ending of the novel which has been criticized as weak. Leo Marx points out that what truth there is in these critics' conclusions does not cover Twain's failure to face the philosophical point of his work. The novel ends weakly because Huck accepted Tom's game playing. Mark Twain, in other words, couldn't turn aside from his milieu. He had to free Jim even though Jim's freedom was meaningless in the context of Tom's shenanigans at the Phelps' plantation.

Lionel Trilling's essay, the "Introduction" to the Rinehart edition of *The Adventures of Huckleberry Finn* is reprinted in Trilling's *The Liberal Imagination*, New York, 1950. Trilling's views and those of T. S. Eliot (in his "Introduction" to the *Chanticleer Press* [Crown Publications] edition of *The Adventures of Huckleberry Finn*, New York, 1950) are discussed by Leo Marx in "Mr. Eliot, Mr. Trilling, and Huckleberry Finn," *American Scholar*, 21 (Autumn, 1953), 423–440.

A large proportion of academic effort and criticism has gone into studies that attempt to deal with the "problem" of the unsatisfactory ending. Most writers in the past 15 years feel that the ending is satisfactory; some feel it is an artistic achievement of the first order. (I can here only cite briefly some - and not always the best or most interesting-representative discussions that concern themselves one way or another with the ending. A quick check into one of the bibliographies listed at the end of the next section will provide the willing student with more material than he can handle.)

Among the better articles is one by Neil Schmitz ("Twain, Huckleberry Finn, and the Reconstruction," *American Studies* [1971], pp. 59–67) which points out that after he is "freed" at the plantation Jim is in the circumstances and conditions of the freed slaves after the Civil War. The analysis Schmitz offers of Jim's condition indicates Mark Twain had a good grasp of his materials.

Chadwick Hansen ("The Character of Jim and the Ending of Huckleberry Finn," *Massachusetts Review*, [1963], pp. 45-66) says that Jim's character is the key to understanding the ending. He is raised from the lowest level of "comic stage Negro" to the highest type of character, the "Natural Man." In the end, when Huck and Jim decide to leave Arkansas, they are escaping from the lowest level of American culture to the last refuge of the "Natural," the Indian Territory. In such terms Hansen sees Jim's escape as a mythic act.

M. J. Sidnell ("Huck Finn and Jim: Their Abortive Freedom Ride," *The Cambridge Quarterly* [1967], pp. 203-211) argues on the one hand that neither Eliot nor Trilling faced up to the problem presented by Jim's treatment at Tom Sawyer's hands, and on the other hand that Marx was too ready to saddle Twain with a superficial sense of morality in opting for the ending. The final chapters, Sidnell points out, contain brutal ironies because Huck and Jim are more enslaved than ever.

Gerald Haslam (*"Huckleberry Finn*: Why Read the Phelps Farm Episode?" *University of Washington Research Studies* [1967], pp. 189-197) indicates the last ten chapters are a fitting ending because they describe the moral dilemma of a slave state.

STRUCTURE

Treatments of technical aspects of composition and structure of *Huckleberry Finn* have focused on a number of topics. Among these is point of view. Two studies by Tony Tanner (Mark Twain and Wattie Bowser," *MTJ* [1963], pp. 1-6; and *The Reign of Wonder*, Cambridge: Cambridge University Press, 1965) and one by Horst H. Kruse ("Annie and Huck: A Note on *The Adventures of Huckleberry Finn*," AL [1967], pp. 207-214) indicate that Twain was aware of the advantages of using a child's point of view early in his career. He knew that such a viewpoint was effective for describing social injustice.

Alan Trachtenberg ("The Form of Freedom in Adventures of Huck Finn," *Southern Review* [1970], pp. 954-971) discusses Huck in his double role as a character in the story and as the teller of the story. Robert Regan's important book-length study (*Unpromising Heroes: Mark Twain and His Characters*, Berkeley: University of California Press, 1965) takes the approach of archetypal criticism in analyzing the characters of Twain's novels, among them Huck.

Analyses of the contrasts between social good and evil, innocence and experience, freedom and enslavement have provided material for many studies. William C. Spengemann (*Mark Twain and the Backwoods Angel*, Kent, Ohio: Kent State University Press, 1965) makes available much information concerning Twain's inability to accept or reject myths of America's innocence. Huck Finn is seen as an ideal innocent initiated into life; the contrast between the river and the shore serves to underscore Twain's attitude.

CHARACTER STUDIES

An unusual study is one by two psychiatrists, Jose Barchilar and Joel S. Kovel. "Huckleberry Finn: A Psychoanalytic Study (*Journal of the American Psychoanalytic Association* [1966], pp. 775-81e) appears to be a thorough, carefully done study which avoids the simplifications, easy generalizations and **cliches** usually found in such studies. The approach may not sit well with many literary scholars, but the article is suggestive.

Tom Sawyer comes in for study in Judith Fetterley's article "Disenchantment: Tom Sawyer in Huckleberry Finn," *PMLA* (1972), pp. 69–74. Fetterley contrasts the character of Tom in the two major Twain novels. She points out that the moral differences between the two Toms indicates a change in Twain's concept of the cruelty the boy perpetrates.

MATERIALISM

Neil L. Goldstein ("Mark Twain's Money Problems," *Bucknell Review* [1970], pp. 37–54) and Elizabeth McMahan ("The Money Motif: Economic Implications in Huckleberry Finn," *MTJ* [1971], pp. 5–10) discuss the use of money in Twain's work. Goldstein focuses on Twain's concern with money and material goods and its contrast with his ideals. McMahan indicates that Huck never lets money get in the way of his feelings in spite of their tightfistedness.

Articles that deal with other thematic concerns are Larry R. Dennis' "Mark Twain and the Dark Angel," in *Midwest Quarterly* [1967], pp. 181–197; and Neil Schmitz' "The Paradox of Liberation in Huckleberry Finn," *Texas Studies in Literature and Language* [1971], pp. 125–136. Schmitz deals with the meaning and application of freedom; Dennis with the fact of death. Dennis feels that Twain handles the problem best in HF because the character of Huck gave him direction.

SENTIMENTALISM

An interesting article that sheds light not only on the novel but also on Twain's philosophical perspective is James B. Lloyd's "The Nature of Mark Twain's Attack on Sentimentality in *The*

Adventures of Huckleberry Finn" (*University of Mississippi Studies in English* [1972], pp. 59-63). Lloyd analyzes the kinds of crying done by the characters in the novel, pointing out that one group of criers is motivated by hate. Twain attacks the sentimental idea that human nature can be improved through appeals to the emotions.

Charles R. Metzger's "*The Adventures of Huckleberry Finn* as Picaresque" (*Midwest Quarterly* [1964], pp. 249-256) argues effectively that Huck has all the earmarks of a picaresque hero. This view should be balanced against that of Henry Nash Smith in his "Introduction" to the Riverside edition of the novel.

Lee A. Pederson's "Negro Speech in *The Adventures of Huckleberry Finn*" (*MTJ* [1965], pp. 1-4) analyzes Jim's speech and concludes that Mark Twain was a careful listener and an excellent recorder.

Finally, one item ought to be noted here as particularly useful. Alan Ostrom's "Huck Finn and the Modern Ethos" (*Centennial Review* [1972], pp. 162-179]) is a clearly written **exposition** of the novel as the account of Huck's inability to break free of the romantic and foolish attitudes and manners represented by Tom Sawyer. This is an excellent review of what is perhaps the most widely accepted view of the novel.

THE ADVENTURES OF TOM SAWYER

CRITICAL COMMENTARY

The best recent criticism of Tom Sawyer has been directed toward illuminating Mark Twain's literary craftsmanship and understanding the sources of some of the details and techniques Twain used in writing the novel. Tom Sawyer is studied as an example of Twain's work before he began writing the triumph of his career, *Huckleberry Finn*.

In his excellent study, Mark Twain and *Huckleberry Finn*, Walter Blair includes a chapter which gives a good general summary of Twain's sources and methods. Blair traces the chronology of the composition of Tom Sawyer, pointing out some of the important details that were drawn from Twain's recollections of his own boyhood and of the local geography of Hannibal, Missouri, which is the prototype of St. Petersburg. He indicates that real-life counterparts of most of the characters and some incidents have been identified with the help of Twain's letters and his Notebooks. But Twain did not merely copy down things as they occurred, or describe people, incidents and places as they existed in real life. He changed details to make the reality suitable for the fiction. Hannibal becomes a shabby village rather than the thriving commercial city it is; many real life characters-Huck Finn's family, for instance-are left out of the story because they don't suit Twain's purposes. He changed names and often modified the personalities of his characters to suit the story whenever he saw fit. Moreover, he added incidents that he had no direct personal experience with; these include the more horror-filled **episodes** in the story. It is obvious, however, that Hannibal had its fair share of the usual crimes of passion that would be found in any city its size, and Mark Twain was likely to have been aware of the murders, rapes, grave-robberies and suicides that occurred during his boyhood. Blair cites three reasons for these changes. First Twain was writing of events that occurred thirty-five to forty years before. It is no wonder he needed to fill in details on which he was vague or which he could not remember. Then, too, there were Twain's well known mood swings. As with all people, much of what Twain remembered depended on the mood he was in. Again, Twain saw things in the light of his present life and his reading. During the 1870s Twain had gotten married and was settling down, so life looked different to him then than it did earlier. And also during the 1870s Twain was being influenced by a great many books he was reading. Blair finds evidence of Twain's reading the dime-novels that were just coming into their own as boy's literature, as well as evidence that Twain was being influenced by writers like Dickens, Wilkie Collins, Harriet Beecher Stowe, - Bret Harte and many others.

And, finally Twain made changes in his raw material because he was, after all, a literary artist who cared about his work and had the skill to impress his personality on a wide variety of material. He practiced at his writing the way actors practice their parts in a play. This was done by writing several different versions of a scene, or by reading his stories to friends and family, or by using material more than once, and so giving it different tone and emphasis at each retelling. By thus learning to control his materials and utilizing them in several different ways, Twain prepared himself for writing the sequel to Tom Sawyer.

Beside Blair's summary, there are many other studies of Tom Sawyer from several specialized points of view. Each of these is an attempt to understand the relationship of this novel to *Huckleberry Finn* or to Twain's conception of humor generally. For instance, Bernard DeVoto gives a chapter of *Mark Twain at Work* to an analysis of Twain's conception of boyhood as it is expressed in Tom Sawyer. Again, Albert Stone, Jr., devotes a chapter of *The Innocent Eye: Childhood in Mark Twain's Imagination* to showing how Mark Twain used the structure of the "Bad-Boy" story as the starting point of his novel. He explains how Twain elaborates details of plot and **theme** to show Tom growing toward maturity.

Another specialized study is Franklin Rogers' book, *Mark Twain's **Burlesque** Patterns*. Rogers devotes part of a chapter to clarifying the relationship between Tom Sawyer and the long tradition of **burlesque** novels in which Twain was writing. He shows how Twain used the **burlesque** as a narrative frame for a series of adventures that would otherwise be disconnected, and concludes that far from being carelessly put together, as has been charged, Tom Sawyer is "one of Twain's most carefully constructed novels...."

Frank Baldanza discusses Tom Sawyer in its relationship to Mark Twain's personality. His study, *Mark Twain: An Introduction and Interpretation*, aims to place each of Twain's works in the context of Twain's biography and social and cultural milieu.

In general these recent studies reflect the change that occurred in Mark Twain studies about 1920. Prior to this time, while Twain was alive, critics often deprecated his works and wondered why he didn't write some of the serious works they knew he had it in him to write. Of course, Twain had his friends among the critics, notably Howells, and he had a large popular following. But from time to time his works were banned from libraries as being "vulgar" or "lacking consequence."

Some years after he died, critics began to be less interested in what he wrote than in why he didn't heed the call to write significant-in their terms-literature. A great many theories were proposed, some of which were the result of the new interest in Freudian psychology that captured America in the 'teens, and some of which were the result of the "anti-patriotic" sentiments that grew up during the same time. Whatever the reason for the surfeit of theorizing, the major problem confronting students for Mark Twain's writings has come to be known as "Mark Twain's Wound."

MARK TWAIN'S ARTISTIC DILEMMA

In 1920 the critic Van Wyck Brooks published a volume entitled *The Ordeal of Mark Twain*. The work is based on Brook's belief that the late-nineteenth and early-twentieth century cultural environment of America was not capable of sustaining artistic minds and helping them to grow and produce works of artistic merit. Brooks' theory, simplified, is that the American cultural scene was too crassly materialistic to produce writers of any significance. He believed that important American literary men had to separate themselves from their native surroundings in order to allow their talents full room for development. Men like Henry James left America for other soils and climates more congenial to intellectual and artistic pursuits. Men like Ralph Waldo Emerson continued to live here, but separated themselves in spirit from strictly American ideals. They refused to restrict themselves to the intellectual attitudes narrowly characteristic of their fatherland.

In addition to these cultural drawbacks, Twain suffered from psychological experiences which left their mark on his sensitive personality. Further, Brooks felt that Mark Twain was a gifted writer, a man with a great talent, but a man who, unfortunately, had never allowed himself to develop his talent fully because he was too involved in the pursuit of more fleeting rewards like riches.

Searching Twain's biography, Brooks and his followers concluded that Mark Twain had chosen to gain popularity among the masses as "America's funny man," rather than to develop his skill as a serious writer. Twain's lifelong pursuit after riches and popularity was based on the not-necessarily-true American belief that wealth plus popularity equals success. That Twain chased riches is evident from the fact that he made much money, which he invested in an unusual and striking house and in business ventures (that often had little chance of success; an indication that Twain was no businessman, what he may have thought to the contrary notwithstanding). He rode to riches more than once in his lifetime. Each time he did so by becoming the darling of the popular audience. In appealing to the mass audience, Twain degraded himself so that he was unable to write the "serious literature" he had it in him to write. Moreover, each time he became wealthy, he gambled his fortune on harebrained schemes to become even wealthier, and ended deeply in debt. The fault here lies with the society which holds up the demon "wealth" as its badge of success.

Brooks and his followers saw other forces as contributing to the repression of Mark Twain's critical artistic skill. Among these were his wife's censorship and delicate artistic prudery, and his friend William Dean Howells' insistence that he had a great comic talent. Not least of the stunting forces were Mark Twain's own boyhood and young manhood days in Southern and Western backwaters among narrow, crude and provincial people - including his own family, who unsuccessfully chased the rabbit of success like a pack of crippled hounds. Writers who agreed with Brooks in his comment were men like Waldo Frank, Malcolm Cowley and Upton Sinclair.

Shortly after the appearance of Brooks' work, however, voices began to be heard in defense of Twain's artistry. These defenders held that far from being corrupted by his surroundings, Twain was helped by them. Mark Twain did not think America was crass and vulgar. Far from it; he considered American democracy and the spirit of free enterprise to be better systems that any the world had ever produced. It is obvious that he would not turn his barbed wit against the institutions he respected most. He did turn it against social institutions he understood to be not honorable and not good. This is as much as we can expect from any man: that he be true to his ideals, whether they correspond to those of his society and age, or not.

Men like Carl Van Doren, Henry Seidel Canby, William Lyon Phelps and Stephen Leacock took issue with Brooks' work. Their criticism ranged from Van Doren's remarks that Brooks had tried to psychoanalyze Twain and had failed, to Leacock's assertion that the West had made Twain an artist, and without the West Twain would have been no artist.

Not until 1932, however, did anyone undertake a full frontal attack on Brooks' position. In that year, Bernard DeVoto, in *Mark Twain's America*, took the position that Twain was a writer of a specific kind of humor: the kind that was found in the works of Petroleum V. Nasby and Artemus Ward, the boisterous local humor of the American West. The loudness and brashness of Twain's work is due to the attitude of the Western frontiersman who not only loved the world and all that he saw in it, but also saw through to the realities of things with eyes uncluttered by the confusing forms that closed up the eyes of more pretentious Eastern writers.

The critical battle lines were drawn between critics who saw Twain as a successful - if superficial - humorist, and those who saw him as a tragic figure ironically hamstrung by the society whose adulation he craved and won.

THE ADVENTURES OF TOM SAWYER

ESSAY QUESTIONS AND ANSWERS

Question: Since it is admitted that *The Adventure of Tom Sawyer* has more than one plot, how can the book be said to be unified?

Answer: Plot is not the only element in a novel that contributes to unity. In the case of Tom Sawyer, unity is achieved by consistent development of the main character. Tom is always the leader in whatever actions - whether mature or childish - he participates in. He functions in many scenes as a teacher of "form" or propriety. For instance, he teaches Becky Thatcher the proper way to get engaged, he teaches Huck about the proper way to go about casting certain enchantments, particularly those requiring an incantation or other special arrangements, and he teaches Joe Harper how to play Robin Hood. He even teaches Sid - by cuffing him - about the impropriety of spoiling people's surprises. This "academic" quality of Tom's personality results mainly from his wide reading. This is but one of the ways in which Twain develops Tom's character consistently in the novel.

He further unifies the novel by narrating the many incidents and episodes involved in it as they relate to Tom. This is particularly true of the scenes burlesquing social institutions and customs.

Tom finds these things personally boring and monotonous, as is evidenced by the **burlesques** of the Sunday-school and the church service.

    Moreover, when Mark Twain describes emotional responses to external things, such as Nature, he keeps his style and **diction** consistent with a boy's point of view. He does not lapse into adult speech when he describes such scenes as the coming of morning on Jackson's Island. The several instances in which Twain uses adult **diction** - for example, the passage describing the villagers' reaction to Injun Joe's funeral - stand out by their very difference from the rest of the book. It is obvious that in these passages the adult Mark Twain is intruding in a child's world.

And finally, Twain keeps the book unified by maintaining unity of theme. The book is ostensibly the story of a boy's coming of age in America, and almost every action in it is directed toward developing this theme.

Question: Contrast Tom Sawyer with his half-brother Sid.

Answer: Tom Sawyer is presented in the first few pages of the novel as a mischievous, fun-loving, ingenious boy. Sid, on the other hand, is presented as an obedient, courteous, good boy. Twain opposes these two several times in the novel and uses Sid as a foil to show Tom in an advantageous light. On several occasions the emphasis that is thus gained is placed on Tom's directness and forthrightness, while Sid is shown to be sly and devious - not worthwhile characteristics. The most striking example of this contrast of characters occurs in the next to last chapter of the novel where we learn that Sid, having overheard the Welshman's plan to surprise the gathering at the Widow's, tells the Welshman's secret, in order to spoil the man's surprise. Tom punishes Sid for this, although he later will attempt to "beat" the Welshman's surprise with one of his own. Tom's action, though, appears more in the character of fair competition than sneaky underhandedness.

The most important thing to note in this contrast is that Mark Twain is playing off the Bad Boy against the Good Boy, and showing that the Bad Boy is basically more moral and humane than the Good Boy. The contrast is not limited to Tom and Sid. It includes the St. Louis sissy whom Tom beats in a fair fight in Chapter I, only to have the sissy heave a rock at him when his back is turned and run home to mother for protection.

Question: How do the horror elements fit into the overall structure of the novel?

Answer: *The Adventures of Tom Sawyer* is a children's book, and as a result it will contain those elements of mystery and adventure that so dearly appeal to children. But on another level, it has been said that these elements reflect adult workings out of the boyhood dreams that Tom so often indulges in.

It is probably most important to regard these elements as parts of the plot necessary to keep the story interesting. For a boy's book must appeal to boys, who are the most adventuresome class of humans on the earth. Even though it has been said that thunderstorms occur whenever Tom is feeling particularly anxious or guilty, the fact remains that thunderstorms - real, two-dollar, gilt-edged thunderstorms, as Mark Twain would say - are particularly horrendous to boys, and at the same time an adventure to be out in.

Mark Twain was not, in the final analysis, particularly devoted to or skilled in symbolic representation of emotions. For this reason among others it isn't likely that the scenes of horror are anything more than an effective literary way of holding attention that Mark Twain learned from the dime-novels which were coming into vogue in his day. The most that can be said about them, therefore, is that they tend to make *The Adventures of Tom Sawyer* something of a literary "potboiler."

Question: Discuss the setting of *The Adventures of Tom Sawyer* as a realistic picture of life in the western United States during the 1840s.

Answer: Mark Twain drew upon his memories of Florida and Hannibal, Missouri and their environs in portraying the setting of this novel. He tells us in the conclusion that man of the people who formed the basis for the characters in the novel were still alive at the time the novel was written, so it is likely that many of the locations for the action also had real-life counterparts. Indeed, it has been proved that places like the novel's Cardiff Hill and Jackson's Island did exist in Mark Twain's boyhood.

But, as he did with the characters, Mark Twain changed the names and many of the details of the elements in the story's setting. There are many reasons for these changes. The most important one is that he had to have these people and places fit into the story as he wanted to write it.

In the main we get a fairly realistic picture of the customs and social institutions of life in small villages. The accounts of religious and academic life, full of **satire** and **burlesque** though they are, give us a good idea of what it was like to go to school and church in those days. The schoolmaster, a petty tyrant and a harsh disciplinarian, was not particularly qualified to lead young minds to an appreciation of intellectual attainments.

And the Sunday School Superintendent was his brother under the skin.

As for the murders, robberies and treasure-troves, well, it is likely that the little village had its share of these. That share was probably no larger than that of a village of similar size and constitution in our day. These particular elements of the novel are more literary devices than objective social reportage.

Question: Describe and discuss Tom's relationship with Becky Thatcher.

Answer: Although Tom is supposed to be engaged to Amy Lawrence, he drops her from his mind the moment he sees Becky, a new girl in town, in the yard of her uncle's house. He doesn't learn who she is until the next day in church school, but he has made enough of an impression on her to have won a sign that she approves of him. This is a flower, which she has thrown over the fence to him. In maneuvering the flower around the corner before he picks it up, Tom acts according to one of the rules in his code of love: it seems there has to be secrecy, a great deal of it, in a love affair. This is emphasized when Tom wins Becky's love after knowing her only three days. He tells her that as part of being engaged they can walk home from school with each other, provided no one is looking. This is **burlesque** of adult love in that it is an overstatement of one of the things adults do when they are in love.

Now, this overstatement characterizes the early stages of the relationship between Tom and Becky. Twain uses the two children as vehicle for his **satire**. But there is a change in the way Twain describes the relationship, particularly in the later chapters of the novel. Once Tom has made peace with Becky by taking her whipping and thus proving himself "noble" - in the best tradition of medieval knight errantry - the love affair settles down to boy-girl friendship. It is described this way in Chapter XXIX when Tom and Becky spend the day playing with their school chums, and in the chapters dealing with the picnic.

But there is also the conversation Tom has with Huck in which he indicates that he will use part of his share of any treasure they find to get married. Huck, in asking Tom who the "gal" is, touches a tender spot; Tom replies it's no "gal," it's a "girl." This kind of protectiveness, which extends to the semantic level, is an indication that Becky has touched some tender feelings somewhere in Tom.

What we have, therefore, in the relationship between Tom and Becky is a relationship that prepares Tom so that he is ready to assume his place in the "civilized" world. That the preparation is effective is indicated by the fact that Tom supports Becky physically and morally when the two of them are lost in the cave. Moreover, as a result of this and other relationships Tom has established in the course of the novel, he is prepared to advance the cause of society to the extent of "ringing" his best friend into it.

Question: Tom's daydreams revolve around books he's read. Is there any significance to the subjects he chooses to dream about?

Answer: Tom daydreams about becoming a pirate or robber or Indian chief. All of these fantasy occupations - when reduced to real world terms - are anti-social. It is fairly clear, then, that Tom is at the stage where he feels a need to rebel against the restrictions imposed upon him by social authority, like his Aunt Polly, Mr. Walters, the Sunday School Superintendent, and Mr. Dobbins the schoolmaster. He does in his dream world what Huck Finn does in reality: he rejects the norms and standards of society, placing himself in the position of a social outcast who is admired by society (as he admires Huck) for being able to live beyond the pale of its shadows.

Of course, in his dream world he sets up standards as strict, perhaps stricter, than those of the society he rejects. He must have things done according to form, or they are meaningless and improper. It is clear, then, that Tom's day dream subjects are chosen because they afford him an opportunity to project his desire to be "individual" and free from social restraint.

THE ADVENTURES OF TOM SAWYER

SUBJECT BIBLIOGRAPHY AND GUIDE TO RESEARCH PAPERS

The research paper should be based on careful reading of the texts of the original works which may be found in numerous editions, including paperback. Six paperback editions of *A Connecticut Yankee in King Arthur's Court* are brought out by the following publishers: Associated Booksellers ("Airmont"); Chandler Publishing Company; Harper and Row, Publishers, Inc.; Hill and Wang, Inc. ("American Century Series"); New American Library of World Literature, Inc. ("Signet"); and, Washington Square Press, Inc. Five paperback editions of *Life on the Mississippi* are available from the following publishers: Associated Booksellers ("Airmont"); Bantam Books, Inc.; Harper and Row, Publishers, Inc.; Hill and Wang ("American Century Series"); and, New American Library of World Literature, Inc. ("Signet"). Three paperbacks contain *The Mysterious Stranger*: *"The Mysterious Stranger" and Other Stories*, published by New American Library of World Literature, Inc. ("Signet"); *The Portable Mark Twain*, published by The Viking Press, Inc. ("Viking Paperbound Portables"); and, *The Complete Short Stories of Mark Twain*, published by Bantam Books, Inc.

There has been a great deal of criticism written about Mark Twain and his works. The following selective items include the most important criticism, with emphasis on *A Connecticut Yankee in King Arthur's Court, Life on the Mississippi,* and *The Mysterious Stranger.* The bibliographical listings have been arranged alphabetically by author for each research topic:

GENERAL: STANDARD CRITICISM AND INTERPRETATION

Questions to consider: Has critical opinion altered since the original publication of these works? Consider the main targets of Twain's **satire**, such as his attacks on the established church and Sir Walter Scott. How is Twain's own personality revealed in these works? In what ways do these books differ from the writing of other authors of the same period?

Baldanza, Frank, *Mark Twain: An Introduction and Interpretation* (1961).

Boynton, Percy H., "Mark Twain," *Literature and American Life* (1936).

Brashear, Minnie M., *Mark Twain: Son of Missouri* (1934).

Brooks, Van Wyck, *The Ordeal of Mark Twain* (1920, 1933).

Calverton, V. F., *The Liberation of American Literature* (1932).

Canby, Henry Seidel, "Mark Twain," *Definitions* (Second Series) (1924).

Cardwell, Guy A., ed., *Discussions of Mark Twain* ("Discussions of Literature" series) (1963).

Chase, Richard, *The American Novel and Its Tradition* (1957).

Clark, Harry Hayden, "Mark Twain," *Eight American Authors: A Review of Research and Criticism*, ed., Floyd Stovall (1956, 1963).

———, ed., *Transitions in American Literary History* (1953).

Clemens, Samuel Langhorne, *Mark Twain's Speeches* (Introduction by Albert Bigelow Paine) (1910).

———, *The Complete Essays of Mark Twain*, ed., Charles Neider (1963).

———, *The Complete Humorous Sketches and Tales of Mark Twain*, ed., Charles Neider (1961).

———, *The Complete Short Stories of Mark Twain*, ed., Charles Neider (1957).

Compton, C. H., "Who Reads Mark Twain?" *Who Reads What?* (1934).

Cowie, A., "Mark Twain," *The Rise of the American Novel* (1948).

DeVoto, B. A., "Introduction," *Portable Mark Twain* (1946).

———, "Introduction to Mark Twain," *Literature in America*, ed., P. Rahv (1957).

———, *Mark Twain's America* (1932).

Ferguson, DeLancey, *Mark Twain: Man and Legend* (1943).

Fiedler, L. A., *Love and Death in the American Novel* (1960).

Foner, Philip S., *Mark Twain: Social Critic* (1958).

Gerould, G. H., "Explorers of Varying Scenes," *Patterns of English and American Fiction* (1942).

Hicks, Granville, "Mark Twain," *The Great Tradition* (1933).

Howard, Leon, *Literature and the American Tradition* (1960).

Johnson, Merle, *A Bibliography of the Works of Mark Twain*, Samuel Langhorne Clemens .... (1935).

Knight, Grant C., "Mark Twain," *American Literature and Culture* (1932).

_____, *The Critical Period in American Literature* (1951).

Leary, Lewis, *Articles on American Literature*, 1900–1950 (1954).

_____, *Mark Twain* (University of Minnesota, Pamphlets on American Writers) (1960).

Lewisohn, Ludwig, *Expression in America* (1932).

Long, E. Hudson, *Mark Twain Handbook* (1958).

Morley, C. D., "Hunting Mark's Remainders," *Streamlines* (1936).

Paine, A. B., *Mark Twain, A Biography* (3 volumes) (1912).

Parrington, Vernon Louis, "The Backwash of the Frontier - Mark Twain," *Main Currents in American Thought* (Volume 3) (1930).

Quinn, Arthur Hobson, *American Fiction: An Historical and Critical Survey* (1936).

Rubin, L. D., Jr., and J. R. Moore, eds., *The Idea of an American Novel* (1961).

Scott, Arthur L., *Mark Twain: Selected Criticism* (1955).

Smith, Henry Nash, *Mark Twain: A Collection of Critical Essays* (1963).

Snell, G. D., "Mark Twain," *Shapers of American Fiction, 1798-1947* (1947).

Spiller, R. E., "Literary Rediscovery: Howells, Mark Twain," in *Cycle of American Literature*, ed., R. E. Spiller (1955).

Spiller, Robert E., and others, eds., *A Literary History of the United States* (1955).

Stovall, F., "Decline of Idealism," *American Idealism* (1943).

Taylor, W. F., *A History of American Letters* (1936).

____, "Mark Twain," *The Economic Novel in America* (1942).

Van Doren, C. C. "Mark Twain," *The American Novel: 1789-1939* (1940).

Wagenknecht, E. C., "Lincoln of Our Literature," *Cavalcade of the American Novel* (1952).

____, *Mark Twain: The Man and His Work* (1935).

Wecter, Dixon, *Sam Clemens of Hannibal* (1952).

A CONNECTICUT YANKEE IN KING ARTHUR'S COURT ANALYZED

Question to consider: In what ways does Twain make a satirical attack on the established church. Discuss Twain's attack on feudalism. Consider the points of view of the several storytellers who relate the story. Note the varieties of literary techniques used in this romance. Is there evidence that Twain is interested in "clothes philosophy"?

Baetzhold, H. G., "The Course of Composition of A Connecticut Yankee: A Reinterpretation," *American Literature* (1961).

Blair, Walter, *Horse Sense in American Humor* (1942).

Brooks, Van Wyck, *The Ordeal of Mark Twain* (1920, 1933).

Canby, H. S., *Turn West, Turn East* (1951).

Carter, Paul, "The Influence of W. D. Howells upon Mark Twain's Social Satire," *University of Colorado Studies* (1953).

Cox, J. M., "A Connecticut Yankee in King Arthur's Court: The Machinery of Self-Preservation," *Yale Review* (1960).

DeVoto, B., *Mark Twain's America* (1932).

Gibson, W. M., "Introduction" to *A Connecticut Yankee in King Arthur's Court* (1960).

Hill, Hamlin, "Introduction" to *A Connecticut Yankee in King Arthur's Court*.

Hoben, John, B., "Mark Twain's A Connecticut Yankee: A Genetic Study," *American Literature* (1946).

Lorch, Fred W., "Hawaiian Feudalism and Mark Twain's *A Connecticut Yankee in King Arthur's Court*" *American Literature* (1958R).

Moore, O. H., "Mark Twain and Don Quixote," Publications of the *Modern Language Association* (1922).

Neider, Charles, "Introduction" to *A Connecticut Yankee in King Arthur's Court* (1960).

Parrington, V. L., *Main Currents in American Thought* (1930).

Quinn, A. H., "Mark Twain and the Romance of Youth," *American Fiction* (1936).

Reiss, Edmund, "Afterword" to *A Connecticut Yankee in King Arthur's Court.*

Roades, Sister M. T., "Don Quixote and A Connecticut Yankee," *Mark Twain Quarterly* (1938).

Scott, A. L., "Mark Twain Looks at Europe," *South Atlantic Quarterly* (1953).

Sherman, Stuart P., "Mark Twain," *The Cambridge History of American Literature* (Volume 3), eds., W. P. Trent and others (1933).

Smith, Henry Nash, *Mark Twain's Fable of Progress: Political and Economic Ideas in* "A Connecticut Yankee" (1964).

Spiller, Robert E., and others, eds., *A Literary History of the United States* (1955).

Taylor, W. F., *The Economic Novel in America* (1942).

Wiggins, Robert A., "A Connecticut Yankee and The Prince and The Pauper: Structure and Meaning," *Mark Twain: Jackleg Novelist* (1964).

Wilson, R. H., "Malory in the Connecticut Yankee," *University of Texas Studies in English* (1948).

Winterich, John T., "Foreword" to *A Connecticut Yankee in King Arthur's Court* (1942).

LIFE ON THE MISSISSIPPI ANALYZED

Questions to consider: Contrast the two parts of the book as to the philosophic point of view of Mark Twain. Why does Twain introduce characters who actually lived? What is the role played by the Mississippi River in this work? How does this work have an inspirational effect on the reader? How does Twain attack Sir Walter Scott?

Cairns, William B., *A History of American Literature* (1930).

Clemens, Samuel Langhorne, "Spring on the Mississippi," in *The American Year*, ed., H. H. Collins (1950).

DeVoto, B. A., "The River," *Mark Twain's America* (1951).

Ganzel, Dewey, "Twain, Travel Books, and Life on the Mississippi", *American Literature* (1962).

Gohdes, Clarence, "Mirth for the Million," *Literature of the American People* (1951).

Kriegel, Leonard, "Afterword" to *Life on the Mississippi* (1961).

Malone, D. H., "Analysis of Mark Twain's Novel Life on the Mississippi," *in The Frontier in American History and Literature*, ed., Hans Galinsky (1960).

Rankin, J. W., "Introduction" to *Life on the Mississippi* (1923).

Schmidt, Paul, "River vs. Town: Mark Twain's Old Times on the Mississippi," *Nineteenth-Century Fiction* (1960).

Scott, A. L., "Mark Twain Revises Old Times on the Mississippi," *Journal of English and Germanic Philology* (1955).

Sherman, Stuart P., "Mark Twain," *The Cambridge History of American Literature* (Volume 3), eds., W. P. Trent and others (1933).

Ticknor, C., "Mark Twain's Life on the Mississippi," *Glimpses of Authors* (1922).

Wagenknecht, Edward C., "Introduction" to S. L. Clemens' *Life on the Mississippi* (1944).

THE MYSTERIOUS STRANGER ANALYZED

Questions to consider: What is the evidence in this work that indicates Twain's pessimism? Does the reader feel sorry for young Satan? Are the **episodes** contrived? Does the ending of the story seem satisfying to the reader? Why was the tale set in the distant past? Is Twain's own youth reflected in this story?

Bellamy, Gladys C., *Mark Twain as a Literary Artist* (1950).

Cowper, F. A. G., "The Hermit Story, as Used by Voltaire and Mark Twain," in *Papers ... in Honor of ... Charles Frederick Johnson*, eds., Odell Shepard and Arthur Adams (1928).

DeVoto, B., "The Symbols of Despair," *Mark Twain at Work* (1942).

Ferguson, DeLancey, *Mark Twain: Man and Legend* (1943).

Fussell, E. S., "The Structural Problem of The Mysterious Stranger," *Studies in Philology* (1952).

Matthiessen, F. O., "Mark Twain at Work," *The Responsibilities of the Critic* (1952).

Parsons, C. O., "The Background of The Mysterious Stranger," *American Literature* (1960).

____, "The Devil and Samuel Clemens," *Virginia Quarterly Review* (1947).

Reiss, Edmund, "Afterword" to "The Mysterious Stranger" and *Other Stories* (1962).

Smith, H N., "Mark Twain's Images of Hannibal," *University of Texas, Studies in English* (1958).

ANALYSIS OF MARK TWAIN AS A PERSON

Questions to consider: Are Twain's Hannibal, Missouri and Mississippi River experiences reflected in his writings? How did his living in the West and his travels in Europe affect his point of view? How did Twain's years of residence in Connecticut influence his writings? Does Twain's viewpoint shift from optimism to pessimism?

Allen, Jerry, *The Adventures of Mark Twain* (1954).

Blankenship, Russell, "Mark Twain," *American Literature* (As an Expression of the National Mind) (1931).

Bolton, Sarah K., *Famous American Authors* (1954).

Bridges, H. J., "Pessimism of Mark Twain," *As I Was Say*ing (1923).

Brooks, Van Wyck, "Mark Twain in the East," *The Times of Melville and Whitman* (1947).

———, "Note on Mark Twain," *Chilmark Miscellany* (1948).

———, *The Confident Years*: 1885–1915 (1952).

———, *The Ordeal of Mark Twain* (1920, 1933).

———, *The Times of Melville and Whitman* (1947).

Canby, H. S., "Homespun Philosophers," *Seven Years' Harvest* (1936).

Chesterton, G. K., "Mark Twain," in *Handful of Authors*, ed., G. K. Chesterton (1953).

Clemens, Samuel Langhorne, "Love Letters of Mark Twain," *Jubilee* (from Atlantic Monthly) (1957).

———, *Mark Twain's Notebook*, ed., Albert Bigelow Paine (1935).

———, *The Autobiography of Mark Twain*, ed., Charles Neider (1959).

Hagedorn, H., "Samuel Langhorne Clemens: 1835–1910," *Americans: A Book of Lives* (1946).

Herron, Ima Honaker, "Mark Twain and the Mississippi River Town," *The Small Town in American Literature* (1939).

Howells, W. D., "Boy of the Southwest," *Jubilee* (from Atlantic Monthly) (1957).

———, "Mark Twain," in "Criticism and Fiction" *and Other Essays*, eds., Clara Marburg Kirk and Rudolf Kirk (1959)

———, "My Mark Twain," in *Shock of Recognition*, ed., E. Wilson (1955).

Hubbell, J. B., "Mark Twain," *The South in American Literature*, 1607–1900 (1954).

Mencken, H. L., "H. L. Mencken on Mark Twain," in *Bathtub Hoax*, ed., H. L. Mencken (1958).

Morris, W., "Available Past: Mark Twain," in *Territory Ahead* (1958).

Priestley, J. B., "The Novelists," *Literature and Western Man* (1960).

Schmittkind, H. T. and D. A. Schmittkind, "Samuel Langhorne Clemens," *Living Biographies of Famous Novelist* (1943).

Untermeyer, L., "Mark Twain," in *Makers of the Modern World*, ed., L. Untermeyer (1955).

Van Doren, M., "Century of Mark Twain," *Private Reader* (1942).

Wagenknecht, E. C., ed., "Little Girl's Mark Twain," *When I Was a Child* (1946).

Wecter, Dixon, *Sam Clemens of Hannibal* (1952).

LITERARY TECHNIQUES USED BY MARK TWAIN

Questions to consider: What was Mark Twain's aim in writing this work? Which are the most effective of the literary techniques he uses? Consider Twain's choice of words and his ability to write good dialogue. Note the unexpected twists of thought in Twain's similes. Is humor introduced for a specific purpose? How is "contrast" used for literary purposes? How does Mark Twain weave recollections of his own past into his material?

Bellamy, Gladys Carmen, *Mark Twain As a Literary Artist* (1950).

Blair, Walter, *Native American Humor* (1937).

Branch, E. M., *The Literary Apprenticeship of Mark Twain* (1950).

Brashear, Minnie M., and Robert M. Rodney, eds., *The Art, Humor, and Humanity of Mark Twain* (1959).

Buxbaum, Katherine, "Mark Twain and American Dialect," *American Speech* (1927).

Canby, H. S., *Turn West, Turn East* (1951).

Clemens, Samuel Langhorne, "Fenimore Cooper's Further Literary Offenses," in *Heritage of American Literature* (Volume 2), eds., L. N. Richardson, G. H. Orians, and H. R. Brown (1951).

____ , "Fenimore Cooper's Literary Offenses," in *Shock of Recognition*, ed., E. Wilson (1955).

____ , "How to Tell a Story" *and Other Essays* (1897).

Cummings, Sherwood, "Science and Mark Twain's Theory of Fiction," *Philological Quarterly* (1958).

DeVoto, B. A., "Critics of Mark Twain," *Mark Twain's America* (1951).

____ , "Mark Twain and the Limits of Criticism," *Forays and Rebuttals* (1936).

____ , "Mark Twain: The Ink of History," *Forays and Rebuttals* (1936).

Fatout, Paul, *Mark Twain in Virginia City* (1964).

Feinstein, George, "Mark Twain's Idea of Story Structure," *American Literature* (1946).

Fraiberg, Louis, "Van Wyck Brooks versus Mark Twain versus Samuel Clemens," *Psychoanalysis and American Literary Criticism* (1960).

Fried, M. B., ed., *Mark Twain on the Art of Writing* (1961).

Gerber, J. C., "Relation Between Point of View and Style in the Works of Mark Twain," *Style in Prose Fiction*, ed., H. C. Martin (1959).

Goold, Edgar H., Jr., "Mark Twain on the Writing of Fiction," *American Literature* (1954).

Hoben, J. B., "Mark Twain: On the Writer's Use of Language," *American Scholar* (1956).

Hoffman, Daniel G., *Form and Fable in American Fiction* (1961).

Krause, S. L., "Twain's Method and Theory of Composition," *Modern Philology* (1959).

Lang, Andrew, "The Art of Mark Twain," in *Mark Twain: Selected Criticism*, ed., Arthur L. Scott (1955).

Lynn, Kenneth, *Mark Twain and Southwestern Humor* (1960).

Marx, L., "The Vernacular Tradition in American Literature," in *Studies in American Culture*, eds., J. J. Kwiat and M. C. Turpie (1960).

Matthews, Brander, "Mark Twain and the Art of Writing," *Essays on English* (1921).

Munson, Gorham B., "Prose for Humor and Satire," *Style and Form in American Prose* (1929).

Phelps, William Lyon, "The American Humorist: Mark Twain," *Some Makers of American Literature* (1923).

Rogers, F. R., *Mark Twain's **Burlesque** Patterns: As Seen in the Novels and Narratives, 1855–1885* (1960).

Rourke, Constance, *American Humor: A Study of the National Character* (1931).

Smith, H. N., *Mark Twain: The Development of a Writer* (1962).

Wagenknecht E. C., *Mark Twain: The Man and His Work* (1935).

ANNOTATED BIBLIOGRAPHY

Texts and Editions

The standard scholarly editions of Mark Twain's writings are in the process of being edited. *The Mark Twain Papers*, a project of the University of California Press, is under the general editorship of Walter Blair, Donald Coney and Henry Nash Smith. This project calls for the publication of fourteen volumes of previously unpublished pieces by Twain, including items he himself rejected as well as business, personal, and literary correspondence. The first three volumes appeared in 1967, and others continue to appear.

John C. Gerber is chairman of the editorial board of the Iowa-California edition of the *Works of Mark Twain*. This series of twenty-five projected volumes is reprinting those works which have been published before.

A full description of these two projects was printed in "Twain in Progress: Two Projects" *American Quarterly* (1964), pp. 621–623.

The early collected edition of most of Twain's writings was edited in 1922–25 by Albert Bigelow Paine under the title *The Writings of Mark Twain*. These 37 volumes are in the collections of most libraries. The edition is flawed by uneven editing, and corrupt and tinkered texts.

The Family Mark Twain, published by Harper and Row, contains most of the major writings in one volume of over 1400 pages. Bernard DeVoto's *The Portable Mark Twain* (New York: Viking Press, 1946, many times reprinted), though old, contains 785 pages of Twain plus an introductory essay by DeVoto.

PAPERBACKS

Paperback reprints of most of Twain's popular works are easy to come by, and many include introductions by critics and scholars. Dell has published a Laurel Edition (1960) of *The Adventures of Huckleberry Finn* with an introduction by Wallace Stegner. Houghton Mifflin's Riverside Edition (1958) has an introduction by Henry Nash Smith. W. W. Norton's annotated edition (reissued 1965) is helpful, as is the Scott, Foresman edition by James L. Bowen and Richard VanDerBeets (1970). Bowen and VanDerBeets print not only the text of the novel, but also a survey by E. M. Branch of the books written about it since the 1940s. They also print forty brief abstracts of critical articles. This is an extremely useful edition.

Hamlin Hill and Walter Blair's *The Art of Huckleberry Finn* (second ed. San Francisco: Chandler Publishing Co., 1969) is a reprint of the first American edition - the preferred copy-text - of the novel. The book also includes almost two hundred pages of introduction and scholarly criticism and comment.

Before making a commitment to use a paperback text of any of Twain's work, you should check two articles: Ruth Stein's "The A B C's of Counterfeit Classics: Adapted, Bowdlerized, Condensed," *English Journal* (1965), pp. 1160–1163; and John C. Gerber's "Practical Editions: Mark Twain's *The Adventures of Tom Sawyer* and *Adventures of Huckleberry Finn*," *Proof: Yearbook of American Bibliographical and Textual Studies* (1972), pp. 285–292. (Abstracted in 1972 MLA Abstracts, vol. I, item 8765.) Both Stein and Gerber note the unreliability of most classroom texts. Stein specifically reports on the use of word-lists and censorship in preparing the texts, while Gerber indicates the texts' general unreliability: there is no text of Tom Sawyer without corruptions, and texts of Huckleberry Finn based on the Author's National or Limp Leather editions contain as many as 2600 variants.

BIOGRAPHIES-GENERAL

Biographies of Mark Twain range from Paine's *Mark Twain: A Biography* (3 vols., New York, 1912), which has the advantages of being an "official" biography and of having been published within two years of Twain's death; to Justin Kaplan's *Mr. Clemens and Mark Twain* (New York: Simon and Schuster, 1965) which has the advantage of having won a Pulitzer Prize. Kaplan's book has practically become the standard biography and supports the general impression of the split between Clemens and Twain.

Jerry Allen's *The Adventures of Mark Twain* (New York, 1954) offers a readable narrative but, like Douglas Grant's *Mark Twain*

(New York: Grove Press, 1962), is less specialized in style and approach than Kaplan's work.

DeLancey Ferguson's *Mark Twain: Man and Legend* (New York, 1943; reissued Indianapolis, Bobbs-Merrill, 1963) has long been one of the best around.

BIOGRAPHIES - JUVENILE

For young readers Monroe Stearns' *Mark Twain* (New York: Franklin Watts, 1965) and Earl S. Miers' *Mark Twain on the Mississippi* (New York: Collier, 1963) are acceptable, though Miers' is fictionalized.

A suggested corrective to Miers is Lucian R. Smith's article "Sam Clemens: Pilot," (MTJ [1971], pp. 1-5), which suggests some reasons why Twain didn't go back to steamboats after the Civil War.

BIOGRAPHIES - LIMITED SCOPE

Some other works give valuable information about specific periods or specific aspects of Twain's life. Dixon Wecter (Sam Clemens of Hannibal, Boston, 1952) provides much information about Twain's childhood in Hannibal. Paul Fatout's *Mark Twain in Virginia City* (Bloomington: Indiana University Press, 1964) does an excellent job of covering the period between September, 1862 and May 1864.

A picture of the Clemens family between 1872 and 1896 is provided in Edith Colgate Salisbury's *Family Dialogues: Susy and Mark Twain* (New York: Harper and Row, 1965). Salisbury uses selections from Twain family writings to provide the dialogue that illustrates their relationships.

Leah Strong recounts the influence of the Rev. Joe Twichell in *Joseph Hopkins Twichell, Mark Twain's Friend and Pastor* (Athens, Ga.: University of Georgia Press, 1965). Twain's relationship with his publisher is documented in Hamlin Hill's *Mark Twain and Elisha Bliss* (Columbia, Mo.: University of Missouri Press, 1964).

Fred W. Lorch, *The Trouble Begins at Eight: Mark Twain's Lecture Tours* (Ames, Iowa: Iowa State University Press, 1968) and Paul Fatout, *Mark Twain on the Lecture Circuit* (Bloomington: Indiana University Press, 1960) are mutually complementary studies of Twain's public speaking career.

PERSONAL ATTITUDES

Margaret Duckett, Mark Twain and Bret Harte (Norman, Oklahoma: University of Oklahoma Press, 1964) indicates that Twain was probably the cause of the trouble between the two writers. Her conclusions are supported by Hamlin Hill's "Mark Twain and His Enemies," (*Southern Review* [1968], pp. 520–529) which notes the importance of fear as a motivating force in Twain's complex personality.

Harold Baetzhold traces Twain's shifting attitude toward England and Englishmen in *Mark Twain and John Bull: the British Connection* (Bloomington: University of Indiana Press, 1970).

Paul Baender suggests that a crucial event in the development of Twain's outlook on life may be a fiction in "Alias Macfarlane: A Revision of Mark Twain Biography" (AL [1965], pp. 187–197).

PERSONAL RECOLLECTIONS

Marilyn Austin Baldwin edited William Dean Howells' affectionate *My Mark Twain: Reminiscences and Criticisms* (Baton Rouge: Louisiana State University Press, 1967). She includes other essays by Howells pertaining to Twain. Justin Kaplan's abridged version of Howells' work, called *Mark Twain: a Profile* (New York: Hill and Wang, 1967), contains essays by other writers. Other personal reminiscences of Mark Twain are provided by Clara Clemens' *My Father, Mark Twain* (New York, 1931).

Finally, but very important, are Henry Nash Smith's *Mark Twain: The Development of a Writer* (Cambridge, Mass.: Harvard University Press, 1962) and Edward Wagenknecht's *Mark Twain: The Man and His Work* (3rd ed. Norman, Oklahoma: University of Oklahoma Press, 1967). Smith discusses Twain as a craftsman and thinker, and illustrates the two sides frequently noted in Twain's personality. Wagenknecht's third edition includes a "Commentary on Mark Twain Criticism and Scholarship since 1960" as well as a bibliography. The book is valuable as a starting point for study of Mark Twain.

The Brooks-DeVoto debate has been summarized in a separate section above, but it should be noted that DeVoto's *Mark Twain's America* (Boston: Little, Brown, 1932) contains a great deal of important background information, as does Brooks' *The Ordeal of Mark Twain* (New York, 1920, rev., 1933, rev. ed. reissued 1970).

HUMOR

Constance Rourke provides background for an understanding of Mark Twain's place in the annals of American humor in *American*

Humor: A Study of the National Character (New York, 1931). Two recent studies also focus on Twain's humor. Pascal Covici, Jr., examines the ways Twain used humor to draw the reader's attention to the human predicament in his *Mark Twain's Humor* (Dallas: Southern Methodist University Press, 1962). *James M. Cox Mark Twain and the Fate of Humor* (Princeton: Princeton University Press, 1965) suggests that Mark Twain was at his best when working according to the "pleasurable principle." Cox's book is quite good.

LITERARY ARTISTRY

Studies of Mark Twain as a literary artist are getting more plentiful. Gladys Bellamy's *Mark Twain as a Literary Artist* (Norman, Oklahoma: University of Oklahoma Press, 1950) set the stage for studies of Twain as an artist. Lewis Leary's *Mark Twain* (Minneapolis: University of Minnesota Press, 1960) and Edgar M. Branch's *The Literary Apprenticeship of Mark Twain* (Urbana: University of Illinois Press, 1950) also deal with the literary artistry of Twain and its development.

An abridged version of Maxwell Geismar's *Mark Twain, An American Prophet* is available from McGraw-Hill (1969) in paperback. The study provides a chronological analysis of Twain's work "in its biographical context" and a critique of Twain as a "literary master and a cultural hero."

In *Mark Twain, Jackleg Novelist* (Seattle: University of Washington Press, 1964), Robert A. Wiggins suggests that Twain was an improviser who did his best work when writing realistic and humorous work. Hamlin Hill shows how Twain's techniques fit a certain kind of publishing operation, the subscription house, which required sensational material

("Mark Twain: Audience and Artistry," *American Quarterly* [1963], pp. 25–40].

LITERARY CRITICISM

A recent full length study of Twain's literary criticism is Sydney J. Krause's *Mark Twain as Critic* (Baltimore: Johns Hopkins Press, 1967).

SOCIAL PHILOSOPHY

As a social commentator, Twain has drawn the attention of many writers. Three important studies are: Louis J. Budd's *Mark Twain, Social Philosopher* (Bloomington; University of Indiana Press, 1962), a broad but complete study of the novelist's social thought; Thomas Blues' *Mark Twain and the Community* (Lexington: University of Kentucky Press, 1970), an analysis of Twain's understanding of the relationship between the individual and his society; and Mary E Goad's *The Image and the Woman in the Life and Writings of Mark Twain* (Emporia State Research Studies [1974], pp. 5–70).

COLLECTIONS OF CRITICAL ESSAYS

Several collections make critical essays available outside library walls. The earliest is Arthur Scott's *Mark Twain: Selected Criticism* (Dallas, 1955). Guy Cardwell's *Discussions of Mark Twain* is in the D. C. Heath "Discussions of Literature" series (1963). Prentice-Hall is represented by Henry Nash Smith's *Mark Twain: A Collection of Critical Essays* (1963) in its "Twentieth Century Views" series, and by Claude Simpson's *Twentieth Century Interpretations of*

Adventures of Huckleberry Finn (1968). All these include useful introductions and carefully chosen discussions.

Frederick Anderson's *Mark Twain, The Critical Heritage* (New York: Barnes and Noble, 1971) reprints 88 reviews and evaluations of Twain from 1869–1913. British and American materials are included.

Lewis Leary's essays are reprinted in his *Southern Excursions, Essays on Mark Twain and Others* (Baton Rouge: Louisiana State University Press, 1971). David B. Kesterson edited *Critics on Mark Twain* (Coral Gables: University of Miami Press, 1973). Dean Morgan Schmitter's *Mark Twain* is a McGraw-Hill paperback in that company's "Contemporary Studies in Literature" series (1974).

BIBLIOGRAPHIES

In addition to the bibliographies and bibliographical notes in the works already mentioned, lists of works about Twain are found in the following:

Abstracts of English Studies. Boulder, Colorado: National Council of Teachers of English. Appears monthly.

American Literary Scholarship/ An Annual, 1963-. Durham, N. C.: Duke University Press. Chapter 5 contains a selective critical bibliography of Twain studies.

Asselineau, Roger, *The Literary Reputation of Mark Twain from 1910 to 1950.* New York, 1956.

Beebe, Maurice and John Feaster. "Criticism of Mark Twain: A Selected Check List." This appeared in the special *Huckleberry Finn* issue of *Modern Fiction Studies* (Spring, 1968), pp. 93–139.

Clark, Harry Hayden and Howard Baetzhold, "Mark Twain" in James Woodress, ed. *Eight American Authors: A Review of Research and Criticism*. Revised. New York: W. W. Norton, 1971.

Leary, Lewis. *Articles on American Literature*, 1900–1950. Durham, N. C.: Duke University Press, 1954.

_____ , et al. *Articles on American Literature*, 1950–1967. Durham, N. C.: Duke University Press, 1970.

MLA Abstracts. New York: Modern Language Association. An annual, publishes abstracts prepared by the authors of the items.

MLA International Bibliography. Vol. I. New York: Modern Language Association. Look under "American Literature IV. Nineteenth Century, 1870–1900. Clemens."

Schmitter, Dean Morgan. "Annotated Bibliography," *Mark Twain, A Collection of Criticism*. New York: McGraw-Hill, 1974.

Spiller, Robert, et al. *Literary History of the United States*. 4th ed. New York; Macmillan, 1974.

www.ingramcontent.com/pod-product-compliance
Lightning Source LLC
LaVergne TN
LVHW021719060526
838200LV00050B/2744